Palm

Easy & Effective Techniques for Reading Palms

(The Complete Guide to Palm Reading Diploma Course)

Travis Fraley

Published By **Chris David**

Travis Fraley

Palmistry: Easy & Effective Techniques for Reading Palms (The Complete Guide to Palm Reading Diploma Course)

ISBN   978-1-77485-677-2

Legal & Disclaimer

The information contained in this ebook is not designed to replace or take the place of any form of medicine or professional medical advice. The information in this ebook has been provided for educational & entertainment purposes only.

The information contained in this book has been compiled from sources deemed reliable, and it is accurate to the best of the Author's knowledge; however, the Author cannot guarantee its accuracy and validity and cannot be held liable for any errors or omissions. Changes are periodically made to this book. You must consult your doctor or get professional medical advice before using any of the suggested remedies, techniques, or information in this book.

Upon using the information contained in this book, you agree to hold harmless the Author from and against any damages, costs, and expenses, including any legal fees potentially resulting from the application of any of the

.ᴄ Of Contents

Introduction

In the United States, many people are fascinated by studying the art of palmistry, also known as Chiromancy. The people who is trying to comprehend the workings of palmistry typically comes from the business world that includes leaders of organizations and entrepreneurs. According to numerous palmistry experts, this group of people want to understand and master the fundamentals of palm reading as it will assist them in their work career, how they communicate with others, particularly when they negotiate and how they select employees, and in general, how to judge any individual who is in contact with them to discover a person's real personality or nature that is beyond their own judgement.

But, in order for students to not get lost in the intricate and complicated guidelines of palmistry it is essential ensure that you learn it in a rational way to construct your process or structure from there.

If you are looking to master this field of study , you must follow a specific system that can aid you in reading palms. The palm reading experts all have an organized method of working that is not just looking at their hands and then read anything that grabs their attention. Most palm reading experts study every aspect of the hand, such that the fingertips, shape of the lines, texture as well as the firmness or softness of the hand, its color, and the general palm, so they see the "bigger image," before going into the details as well as "connecting those dots" to make an understanding.

Before you can read and understand the fundamentals of palmistry, or how it operates it's essential that every student possess an open mind or a mindset that is open to possibilities. If you believe you're the type of person who isn't able to accept anything without proof or is always doubtful about the way things function I would suggest that you should quit reading this and go to a different book, possibly one with an academic theme.

This is due to the fact that palm reading, despite of its long-standing history has not been nor will it ever be a reality or a precise science. There is no evidence to prove that it actually works (or is it not) however it's not even backed by tests conducted by scientists, that is why the subject is regarded as a possibility, but this doesn't mean palmistry isn't completely true or even true. Perhaps it is something that our ancestors came up with years ago to explain a myriad of phenomena or was simply born because of boredom, but nobody knows for certain.

It's an art form that's endured the years and has been passed down through several generations and has in some way or other, changed the way the lives of people. There may be occasions when you can connect a personal situation to a predictions made by palm reading, but it could be simply a coincidence or could be a real thing or not. Being open to new possibilities when learning about this art is crucial to fully comprehend the way in which it functions. But, regardless of whether individuals or experts view chiromancy as something that is real or merely the result of imagination the present or future, as well as the character of a person is entirely within the mind. Be aware that your fate is not dependent on what's written on the palm of your hand but on you. In the words of W.E. Henley famously stated, "I'm

the master of my destiny; I'm the master in
my own soul."

Chapter 1: What Is Palm Reading?

Reading palms involves a combination with looking closely at both the fingers, the hands along with the lines and mounts and marks on the palms and paying attention to your instincts, every aspect you see on the palms can be taken as a whole, an experienced palm reader takes into account all lines, marks and mounts, and interprets them together.

Have you ever thought about the fact that there are no two hands are alike and that no two palms have the same? The palms on your two hands are distinct. They might look similar, but they'll be distinct.

Palmistry isn't about "how long will I live or making dramatic answers, it's about understanding and working with the positive qualities and potential of someone that are evident by the various markings on their hands.

What are the things you require to be able to read palms?

There is nothing you need to start the first hand reading, with an open mind and the desire to learn are the primary elements.

Equipment

A notebook and a pen. The notebook you use frequently to document your experiences and also as a reference book. As time passes, your notebook will develop into a personal record of everything you've learned , and will serve as a handy reference guide that you will likely refer to frequently.

Some volunteers. It shouldn't be difficult since a lot of people are curious to learn more about the movements that their fingers make. Inform your volunteers that you'd like them to serve as your study subjects as you build your confidence and discover more concerning the palm. It is essential to assure your participants that all information you observe in their palms and in your notebook is protected.

A non-judgmental and calm approach. When someone is having an experience with a palm reader, they may be anxious, particularly when it is the first time they have encountered an expert in palm reading. They might be glued to every word you say , and interpret your every gesture according to their own interpretation. Many people fear they'll hear that they're about to die or face an awful fate. So, take the time to inform your loved ones that this information is not given through a palm reading, and we do not are able to predict our death date!

A few years ago, I gave an hand reading to a friend of mine. I stopped for a few minutes longer than I normally would while performing the reading. I saw an unusual mix of lines. Nothing bad and just a bit unusual. However, my friend began to panic and asked 'what was I seeing when I explained that I took a while to process the mix of lines before explaining the lines to him and I wasn't finding anything of a negative nature. I assured him of the fact that nothing was wrong and there wasn't anything to worry about.

A palm reading can be very thrilling however, it could be a source of anxiety for certain people It is the responsibility of the person reading to do so with compassion and care.

The study of the shape and the sensation of the hand

Before you are able to identify the lines and marks on your palms, you need to learn to know the entire hand. Each hand is unique.

Each hand has a distinct texture and colour and each hand has its own appearance and feel.

The dominant hand

It is that which a person writes with. It informs about the present moment and the way a person uses their skills as well as providing information about how they are using the talents and skills they were born with.

The non-dominant hand

The non-dominant hand provides details on the past, an individual's inheritable traits and how those possible traits can be utilized and developed to improve the future opportunities.

Examine your own hands. Then ask your fellow volunteers whether you could take a look at their hands after conducting an extensive examination, you can note down the following information.

Shape and size

Examine the hands' size. Are they large, small, or average in comparison to the rest of your body Are both hands similar in size or is one bigger over the other? Take note of the shape of each hand.

The five types of shapes recognized in palmistry are the square spatulate, conic, spatulate pointy/psychic, and mixed.

Here's a short description of each

The palm is square , and the fingers are about longer than the hand with the sharp tips. Keywords: practical, well-structured and well-organized. Sometimes, it is referred to as the practical hand.

Conic hand, slightly tapered in the middle and with rounded or tapered fingers. Key words: creative, intuitive, and enthusiastic. If the fingers are tangled, the person typically has endurance strength. Most often, it is the hands of females.

Spatulate hand: fingers are an splayed look, similar to spatulas. Key words: active entrepreneurial and grounded.

The hand with the point is A delicate hand that has large fingers as well as pointed fingers The hand features delicate and delicate line marks. Key words: dreamy introspective, spiritual, impressionable. The hand design is pretty uncommon.

A mixed hand This hand is not in all of the description mentioned above but includes a mix of different hand shapes I've described. Key words: flexible as well as adaptable, likable. This is the shape of your hand that you see more often in the readings of your hands.

Note if one hand is different from the other in shape, size or feeling it could mean the existence of two different sides to the individual's personality and character or how they conduct their daily life.

In your notebook, write down the shape you think the palm of the person you are studying is wearing. Keep in mind that this is your notebook. You are creating a record of what you think, observe and describe the palm you're taking a look at.

Complete the notes as much as you can, this helps you remember the particular palm you were using as you review your notes.

Don't be worried If you're unable to decide on the shape of your hand. Being a novice, it is not necessary to place too much emphasis on the shape of your hand. It is only one element of the process of reading palms. The most common hand you'll meet is the mixed hand, keep in mind that a palm reading considers every part of the hand as the whole.

It is also possible to notice that when you start taking palm prints that the form appears to be different to the 3D palm. This is why thorough note-taking will give you an useful and precise details.

Lines

Do the lines on palms smooth and difficult to discern or are they strong and deeply etched or between? There are many lines, or only some? Lines of fineness are usually found in the palms of people who are sensitive. The more prominent lines are on the confident palm. Do these lines match with your knowledge of the palm of the person you are studying?

Touch

Take a look at the back of your hand, and note the sensations, cool/warm dry/damp, firm/soft and firm, then flip the hands around and repeat the evaluation on the palms. What color are the hands? Are they light, red or are they blotchy, red, etc?

Keep a notebook in which you write more notes on the hands of the person whom you examined.

Include the following details.

Today's date. Name of the person. The date of their birth. Sex. Marital status. Children. The career, both past and present. Any health issues that are known to be present.

Explain how the information you have about their character is in line to the evaluation made by them.

As you begin reading palms by using the case studies of those who are known to you will assist you tremendously. As you look over the information that you've gathered and you'll be able to assess how accurate the information that you read from your palm and how it connects to the palm of the person you are studying. This will help you gain confidence when you decide to look at the palms of other people.

The handshake test.

A simple handshake can tell something about someone and is an acceptable method to touch someone who is completely stranger and learning something about the person. It's a way to introduce yourself when you offer the hand of someone you're providing them with a glimpse of the character of you.

Handshake hands with relatives and friends Does their handshake show their character? For example do the handshakes of your great aunt match her stoic and uncompromising attitude to life? How about your timid nephew? Does his handshake feel unsteady and uncertain? And your brother who is caring is his handshake warm, loving and confidence?

While walking around make sure to shake hands with the most people you can. Check their handshakes. Was it firm and solid, inspiring confidence, or was it strong and firm enough to cause concern or was it gentle and gentle or gentle and weak?

In your notebook, note the way their hand shake was like and how it compares to the kind of person they were. Also, record the details and the context of the discussion you had. Be as descriptive as possible.

It could be something like this: (1) Mr. Jones received me with a firm handshake. I was able to sense that he was happy to meet me. I was confident of the appointment and his capacity to assist me. (2) Or I could write that Mr. Jones shaken my hand and smashed my fingers, I'm concerned that I might be a bit too stern. (3) Or the other option is that Mr Jones accepted me with a gentle, non-committal handshake. He appears somewhat distracted, and this didn't inspire confidence.

The knowledge gained from this course will prove invaluable as you progress and discover more about the palm, hand and what it says about the person's personality and character.

Palm watching

It's a lot like watching people, but the focus is on palms. You will discover many details about someone, information that they are not conscious of sharing.

When you are watching television documentaries or the news, people often give their hands towards the camera when they are talking or waving.

Check each palm you encounter If the person you are looking at is famous, you're likely to be aware of their past and their lives. Check if what you know is apparent in the hand they are holding and note whether the palm is closed or open and take a close look at the main lines. Does reflect the image they portray to the public?

It is also possible to watch people that you meet in everyday day life. Check if their attitude is apparent in their posture or place their hands.

Are their hands together? are they nervous? Are they using their hands to signify and emphasize the words they're using Do they think they feel confident? It could be that they are covering their hands. Does the way they look reflect this?

Keep notes in your notebook as you continue to create your profile of what this signifies to you.

Concerning palm prints

As I began my reading palms, I realized that the best method to increase confidence and get information was to get lots of people to provide me with palm prints. I asked all my colleagues at work and also my husband's coworkers to give me palm prints. The person

I asked was known to me by an identifier and I was informed whether they were female or male. I didn't know who the prints were belonging to. This method helped me collect several prints filled with interesting information.

My own time and without any pressure, I was able look for the meanings of lines that I have in my hand reading books. I was able to evaluate the dominant and non-dominant hands in depth and utilize an accurate ruler to measure the length of fingers.

I then created an individual reading of each print. Each reading was then handed by me back to the printer's owner. I am waiting for their feedback.

There were some interesting responses. Some thought I accurately described the events while others felt I was far off!

A particular incident is etched in my memory. I wrote a report on an accurate palm reading for the male. The only thing I'd received was that I had the palm of a man in his mid-thirties.

I was working my way through the palm print step-by- stage, and I recorded specifics of the main lines and mounts, as well as the combinations of them.

As I examined the line and mounts, I could tell that the subject seemed to be little bit of a "one woman's girl. His palm was a sign of many affairs and maybe a problem in committing to just one person. I didn't know whether this person is married, or not. I wrote the report carefully , highlighting possible issues with honesty and integrity and I awaited to hear back.

I received a short quick response that told me straight up that I was completely off with my understanding of the palm. I was okay because I was just a novice and errors were bound to happen. But, six months later, it was revealed that the man was engaging in an affair with his wife behind her back and was furious at the fact that I had noticed it.

The only time I've observed that people aren't satisfied with having their palms examined is when they have something to keep from!

Taking palm prints.

There are a variety of methods I have used to make palm prints.

* Paper and ink.

* Lipstick (this is actually effective)

* Making use of the photocopier

* Making use of an electronic camera

Paper and ink

To print a photo with ink, you'll need an excellent quality paper and the ink pad (non-permanent). Request the person taking the print you want to take their palms into the pad to fill every inch of the palm area with. After that, you need to press the person's hand onto the paper while trying not to scratch the paper. Make sure to do this on both hands. Inscribe the date, as well as beside the prints the name of the person's age and sex. You can also note which palm is left print, and which is the left palm print.

Lipstick

To print a photo with lipstick, you'll need an excellent quality piece of paper as well as a dark-coloured lipstick. Red appears to be the most effective. Place the hands of the person who is taking the prints you're taking with the lipstick. Request the person to press their palms together in such a way that the lipstick will get into every crease and crevices. Apply their hands to paper and write down the date, and then beside each print, write the person's name age, sex and age, and what is the left palm print , and which prints on their right.

Photocopier

Utilizing a scanner or photocopier is among the simplest ways to do so. It's not messy and creates beautiful crisp prints that are easy to read and to save. If the printer is big enough, place two hands over it. For smaller ones, just one hand at a. Note the date, the person's name , age, and sex, as well as which hand print is left and which that of the palm on the right.

Utilizing an electronic camera

Today, this is the most effective method to print your photos You can capture high photographs using a camera or a smart phone.

To achieve this, make sure that you are in good lighting in the shade far from the direct sun and also keep your hands as straight as they can be.

If possible , I would like to print and take photos or photocopies of palms. Photos and photocopies are simple for me to manipulate and offer an idea of the hand's form and typically show the main lines and the lipstick print provide more details of the fine lines.

Racettes are a type of bracelet that sits located at the base of the palm . On the inside of the wrist. take note of the number of apparent and if they're sharply arched or straight curly. The typical number is anywhere between 1 and 3.

Make sure to keep your palm prints in a secure place. If you can keep a record of your palm prints every five years, you're likely to notice slight changes in the lines of your palm shift over time, reflecting the changes that occur in the life of a person.

The thumbs are being examined

Indian palm readers believe that the thumbs to be more important than fingers. They consider that the thumbs have most of the information within the palm of a person.

When I practice reading with my palms I find the thumb is extremely significant, however like I always say that no part in the hand or marking in the palm must be considered as a whole. As a reader, you want at the whole picture considering every part of the palm you're viewing.

The lines and the mounts of the thumbs are full of information on our health, our life's ups and downs, as well as our friendships as well as how we handle stress, and how our constitution is generally

Examine the thumbs of as many people as you can. Write an in-depth report on each thumb of the participants.

The thumb region is protected in the lifeline. We will examine this line, as well as the stress and friendship lines that lie within the life line in the future.

Thumb is split into 3 parts The three sections represent willpower, logic, and love.

If you take a look at the image, you'll notice that the thumb digit contains two roughly equal sections . One represents will power and the second representing logic. Alongside these sections, at the top of the thumb, and reaching to the palm, can be found it the Mount of Mars and the Mount of Venus, as its name implies, the Mount of Venus gives

21

information about love. The long arched line that runs to the left of the Mount of Venus is known as the life line.

Should the thumb's top portion of the thumb that represents the individual's will power, be the bigger of the two sections it would suggest that the person is extremely strong willed and can achieve what they decide to achieve and will not be deterred away from their objectives.

If someone is born with only a small amount of willpower, they may have a difficult time trying to commit to a choice or lifestyle choice, but they are able to achieve it, but it's likely to be a lot more work than someone with more of a will.

If the lower section that is a representation of logic, is the smaller of the two the person is likely to make quick, sometimes impulsive choices, and is likely to believe that if you feel it's right, then it's right'.

A person who has a bigger mental section is more likely to be slower to arrive at a decision, as they weigh all the advantages and disadvantages. They're not likely to be highly impulsive.

The Mount of Mars represents the level of courage that a person is, a flat-mounted mount typically indicates someone who doesn't always believe that they can be successful, they may struggle to face up against others , and they might lack confidence in their abilities.

A heightened sense of the mount may be a sign of someone who is confident and, at times, domineering. A full and fleshy Mount of Mars is usually held by a confrontational, and even aggressive individual.

The Mount of Venus is the huge area located that lies at the base of the thumb. This space represents the ability of a person to be loved and to love. It is evident from the image that the mount is average in size It is not the top or flat, which indicates a typical love for oneself. If the Venus mount Venus is large and fleshy, then the individual is most likely to be a an interest in every aspect of the good life, which includes a potential excessive desire for food and drinks. A larger mount is usually taken care of by very pragmatic people who appear as unrestrained or distant because they usually prefer to keep their feelings secret.

23

Horizontal lines running over an area called the Mount of Venus are thought to symbolize the people that a person makes throughout their life. The longer the line, the more a friendship is strong. Many delicate lines on this mountain can be a sign of a nervous state.

The family ring has a chained line that sits at the bottom of the thumb and separates your thumb and the Mount of Venus. If the chain is well made and has a distinct chain pattern it indicates the individual is a strong family member and family ties.

The angle of the thumb can reveal a wealth of information about a person's personality. In this case, the angle is approximately 45 degrees. This person is confident and has faith in themselves. If the angle of the thumb towards the palm was 90 degrees, then you'd be looking at a confident personwho is happy with their life and willing to try new things, a higher angle indicates that they are not confident enough. If the thumb is held in close proximity to the hand, the person may not have confidence in their abilities and lacks confidence in their abilities to succeed If the thumb is hidden in the palm of the hand, the person will likely be nervous and shy.

Keep a notebook.

Take note of the way people hold their thumbs with respect with their hands. Take a look at your relatives and friends take note of how the thumbs are held in different ways in relation to the way they feel in that particular moment.

Check out photos of people who are in the spotlight. If their thumbs are kept with their thumb pointing away from the hand, they will feel confident and content If a thumb is hidden behind the palm of someone's hand might indicate they're feeling nervous or unsecure and are not content with their current situation at this moment. A thumb that is hidden is like hiding a piece of one's persona. Consider a time when you felt uneasy or worried most likely put your thumb in your palm.

Children and babies frequently place their thumbs in their mouths to soothe themselves and also when they are ready to sleep.

The fingers

When looking at the fingers, it is crucial to observe the non-dominant hand first . then compare it to the fingers of the dominant hand (the one used to write). Then, you will be able to discern how the individual uses and applied the characteristics that they were born with which are displayed in the hand that is not dominant as well as the traits they've developed on the dominant hand.

You're likely to be amazed by the amount of information you will discover about yourself or the person you're researching, just by looking at your finger.

Look at your hands face-up, and determine the names of each finger.

The image above illustrates the hand that has average lengths of fingers. A majority of the hands you see are average, so take note of any distinctive features to narrow your focus.

The index finger or first fingers is also known by the name of Jupiter.

The middle finger or the second fingers is known as the finger Saturn.

Ring finger referred to as the finger of the Sun and Apollo.

The little finger is also known by the name of Mercury.

Middle finger or the fingers from Saturn is the one that balances the hand. It is also the longest finger. It's a crucial reference point for looking at the fingers.

Like in the case above Jupiter and Apollo/Sun typically are approximately identical in length.

Mercury typically extends to close to the bottom portion on the Apollo finger. This could be a difficult finger to read since you have to alter the length of comparison because of the downward slope that the palm. This is accomplished by measuring the Mercury finger and comparing that measurement with Apollo's finger. Apollo.

Each finger needs to assess its size with the non-dominant hand as well as its size with respect to other fingers.

In determining the length of fingers, and also as an indicator of what the fingers are shorter or long the fingers typically reach around half way into the upper portion of the larger finger it is located next to.

Sometimes, you'll meet someone whose fingers are noticeable shorter or longer when they are on the one hand and the other.

If the hand that is not dominant has fingers that are longer than the other two hands, the individual is likely to possess many talents and qualities, but they may be uncertain about their abilities to achieve success and may lack confidence. If the dominant hand has longer fingers, they're likely to be confident in all aspects of their lives.

Let's begin with the finger that is next to your thumb. Jupiter.

Jupiter finger - confidence, assertiveness, taking risks.

One finger in particular, Jupiter shows how confident someone is confident, how assertive they are able to be, and what they do with these qualities in their everyday life. The larger your finger is Jupiter indicates how confident, and an entrepreneur the person could be.

If the non-dominant hand is one of the fingers that is short of Jupiter and that hand of the dominant has a shorter finger of Jupiter the person who is in question might prefer not to

28

take risk in their life. They might be cautious with money, and cautious about life and require a sense of security to be satisfied.

If the hand that is not dominant is short in the Jupiter finger while your dominant hand sports a lengthy Jupiter finger, it indicates someone has put in a lot of effort to increase their confidence and confidence in their abilities.

If on the hand that is not dominant, that the index finger Jupiter is larger than the one for the dominant hand that person has potential hidden to develop confidence, however they may not always have faith in themselves, they might have been stifled in their younger years, but they have the potential to be successful later on in life.

In the event that the predominant Jupiter finger is particularly long it's likely to belong to someone who has a lot of confidence and extraordinary leadership abilities.

If both dominant and non-dominant fingers on Jupiter are nearly as long (or nearly so lengthy) than that of the Saturn finger, the person who owns it could be considered a risk-taker throughout their lives.

If fingers Jupiter are of average length, and is comparable to the Apollo/Sun fingers, the person who owns them will be of average levels of confidence.

Saturn finger - balance.

As mentioned previously, the middle finger Saturn is the point of balance of the hand.

Long Saturn finger could be a sign of someone who would like things done in a particular way and they may be dominating by their desire to accomplish their objectives.

A shorter, non-dominant Saturn finger as well as a long dominant Saturn finger could manifest as those who are at odds with their personal dreams and goals. They might never be content with the things they have accomplished in their lives and always seek to achieve more.

Someone with a small finger Saturn on their dominant hand is usually an independent person They are able to dance to their own drum , but they may require a lot of willpower to keep their focus on every aspect of their life.

A typical length Saturn finger belongs to those who are well-balanced in all aspects of their life.

If one fingers of Saturn be slanted to the hand that belongs to Apollo the person will likely be at odds with the way they'd like to live their lives and the way others expect them live their lives.

Sun/Apollo finger - imagination emotional, love, and emotion.

It is the finger located on the left hand on which engagement and wedding rings are worn traditionally. Prior to modern developments in medical science and understanding of the way the body works and functioned, the majority of people were of the belief that there was a vein which went through the Apollo fingers directly into the heart. This is believed to be the main reason Apollo finger was selected to wear engagement and wedding rings.

It is important to note that men tend to have a bigger Apollo/Sun than Jupiter finger when compared to women. Keep this in mind while doing your analysis. This could be due to men having more testosterone exposure while in the womb.

The sun/apollo finger represents the person's attitude towards life as well as love and commitment, and also the artistic side of their personalities.

A non-dominant, short Sun finger, when paired with a dominant long finger is a sign that someone is working hard to improve their the ability to think creatively in their lives.

A long , non-dominant Sun finger as well as a shorter or average dominant Apollo finger may suggest that a person is a hidden talent waiting to be discovered. Make sure the person knows that these abilities can be developed through determination and dedication.

A dominant ring that is overly long finger (as as long as the fingers from Saturn) is an indication of a gambler throughout their lives. They'll go to any length to achieve what they want, however the person might not have commitment.

A small Sun finger could be a sign of a selfish or weak nature.

Studies have revealed that those who have a larger that the typical Sun finger on their dominant hand are more proficient in maths and Physics.

Mercury finger - language and communication.

You'll need to apply the measurement method previously mentioned to determine whether you are able to determine if the Mercury finger is short, long or average. Mercury generally extends about the level of just above the upper portion on the Apollo finger. This could be a difficult finger to determine since you have to alter the length of comparison because of the downward upwards slope in the palm. The method is to measure the Mercury finger, then comparing the measurement with Apollo's finger. Apollo.

The mercury finger is a reflection of the entire spectrum of language and communication in our lives. It could be the spoken word or language, written word and the language that we love!

Someone with a dominant long Mercury finger is likely possess an artistic or creative personality. They could be musical, if that is the case, the thumb is likely to be curved at the point of the thumb's base.

People with fingers that are long Mercury fingers are usually adept at communicating through either written or spoken words and are skilled at creative writing.

People with dominant long Mercury fingers usually do well in dealing with money.

Extremely long Mercury fingers are commonly found on the hands actors and people of the flamboyant type.

A small Mercury finger could be a sign of someone who doesn't want commitment and prefers to stay young and never to get older and accepting any type of obligation.

If the bottom on the Mercury fingers is solid, the person is likely to be focused in their thoughts about their life.

In general, when the bases of any fingers are soft and fleshy , the person tends to indulge in excess.

Notebook: Note the length of fingers and proportions on the hands of friends and people you watch on TV, and also by looking at pictures from magazines and newspapers.

34

Take note of the various variations and take notes on how they relate to the person's personality and the way they present them to other people.

Rings are worn to symbolize love.

It is fascinating to observe the fingers that people put rings on and how it is a reflection of their character and style.

The following ring names are taken from books I've read as well as my own observation of rings that are worn and the way they reflect and show a part of one's personality.

It is not always obvious that when we wear rings that it could be an expression of fashion as well as a personal statement to convey something to the world at large about us.

A ring that is worn on the thumb may be a sign of someone who is determined to have control at all times . It can appear to be extremely dominating. The presence of a ring around the thumb can be a strong indication that the wearer is looking to be perceived as important and successful.

A ring that is worn on the wrist of Jupiter signifies that someone is confidentand is able to stand up for themselves and reach their goals and fulfill their goal of becoming "the boss".

A ring that is worn by the hand of Saturn could be a sign to the world that "I'm balanced." Or it could be a subconscious effort to create balance in their lives. The ring worn on this area shows that the wearer is focused on concerns of emotional and personal security.

A ring that is worn on the sun/apollo finger is a reflection of issues of love and the heart. It is the finger traditionally used to wear rings for engagement or wedding. Rings on this finger makes it clear that the individual is involved in an intimate relationship. A ring that is worn on the non-dominant ring finger may indicate a desire for affection and friendship.

Rings on the finger of the ring could be a sign of "I'm in a relationship or partnership, and I want to share my experience to all the people of this world'.

A ring that is worn around the wrist of Mercury is a sign of keen interest in all aspects of business and communication. The larger the ring , the greater the signal to the world about how the person is able to convey their message!

If a person is not wearing any rings, they is a sign that they don't want to divulge all of their thoughts or their character to the world at this moment in their lives.

You'll be able make your own idea of what wearing rings signifies to you and what significance, or lack of important, they are to the analysis and reading of the palm.

The history behind the two-finger gesture

When researching this book, I found this tiny bit of history that I found extremely interesting. There's some disagreement about the origins or even the authenticity of the story, since numerous archers captured were held for ransom or even killed.

I found the story interesting and worthy of telling

The insulting gesture that involves raising two fingers of Jupiter and Saturn in a V-shape The 'archers salute' is believed to go to the century-old of war, a string of battles that took place over the period 1337-1453, between and the House of Plantagenet as the head of the Kingdom of England and the House of Valois who were the ruling the Kingdom of France.

The English were great shooters with Long bows as well as archers. According to legend, should an English bowman were caught by a Frenchman, his bow fingers would be severed to stop the bowman from drawing his long bow at the French. It was the most severe accident an archer could sustain as he was totally disabled and unable to be a part of the war with his bow and archer.

Anyone English archers who hadn't been captured could taunt their adversaries by showing two fingers to prove they were still alive and capable of firing the bow and arrow.

The main lines of the palm

In this chapter, we'll examine the primary palm lines, those that most people know about These include:

The line of the heart.

The line of the head.

The lifeline.

The line of fate.

It is interesting to consider that the palm lines begin to develop in the womb during 12 weeks gestation. This suggests that a part of our personality is already formed before we're even born. As we get older, our palm lines alter in response to the transformations that take place in our lives.

The heart line

The heart line contains information on relationships, emotions and the heart's physical structure.

Keep your hand in place with your the palm looking towards the upward direction. When you look at your palm, the long line that extends across the top just below your fingers is the heart line.

The heart line begins at the outer edge of your palm below the small finger, and continues across the palm to the first finger.

On certain palms, the line is long and straight, while in other palms it's more long and curves upwards to the center of both the second and first fingers.

In general, the more curving the line, the more emotional or capable of showing emotion, the person who holds the palm is. The closer the end of this line is between your first and second fingers and the more capable the person is to express the love of others. It could mean that the person is extremely generous and open or is extremely dependent on others to ensure their happiness.

Someone with a straight heartline may struggle to express themselves or keeping their feelings in the back of their mind They are usually calm and unaffected by emotion.

The emotional turmoil of major magnitude appears in this line as tiny bubbles. The size and length of the bubble reveals the severity and length of the tense moment. If you notice an individual or two and you want to inform the owner that you're witnessing a period of stress that occurred in their past. If there are more than one, you are able to estimate how closely these events were by the distance they appear in the distance.

If the heart is able to send an artery down to meet the line of the head, this could be a sign that those who make decisions are typically governed more by the heart than by the head.

It is along this line that symptoms for heart attacks or disease may show. If the person who owns the palm suffered an incident of heart disease, you could observe a slight crack, star, or a an interruption in the line. If you take a look at the line of life, you will likely find the same mark, roughly the same distance across the line.

If I notice such a mark, I usually say that I'm noticing signs of possible health issues At that point, the person I am reading will usually inform me about any health issues that have occurred recently. If they're unaware of any health issues one of the main points to remember is that when a person makes changes to their lifestyle, this will show in their health as well as the palm's lines that is the one with these markings. The owner of the palm that has these marks can change as well as improve his health as well as their future.

The head line

The head line provides details about mental stability, the way an individual copes with stress and be a sign of any issues with depression.

The head line runs directly beneath that of the heart line. It begins beneath the first finger across the palm, and will end about 3/4 of the palm.

There are times when you come across a person with an asymmetrical head and heart line that appear to join together into one. This is referred to as an individual palmer line.

The single palmercrease could be used to define two different things.

The medical field has known for a long time that children diagnosed with Downs syndrome have only one line that replaces the heart line as well as the head line. It is located right across of the palm, from one palm side to the opposite.

If the single palmer crease is visible on your palm or on the palm of someone that you are looking at it's a strong indicator that those who have the palm crease tends to be focused and determined to reach their goals and attain their personal goals. If you look up Google will reveal it is the case that Tony Blair, Hilary Clinton and Robert de Niro all have one palmar crease. which is a powerful symbol indeed!

A head line that slopes sharply downwards to the palm may suggest depression issues or a lack of ability to cope with stress.

A few years ago, while I was doing an analysis of the palms of an unidentified young woman I noticed the headline was sending an extremely fine offshoot in her palm. I talked about what I saw with her and asked whether she was experiencing anxiety or stress at the moment. She explained that she was going through difficulties and was very down and was unsure if she could ever bounce back'. After telling her that this would not last forever and that her lines were likely to change with her changing and, reassuring her that nothing is exactly the same. She was reassured. When I visited her again a few years later, she informed me that she was in a far happier place, that her life had improved and changed and a close look at her hairline revealed less fine lines that drooped.

Straight head lines typically is the sign of a person who is calm and is able to handle everything life throws at them. They typically possess a rational approach to all situations and are able to figure things out.

A straight and short head line is usually seen on business people who is likely to be a single-minded person and committed to achieving whatever goal they have set.

If the head line ends with a fork, it is a good sign of that you are a highly creative and active brain. It is possible to find this symbol at the fingertips of writers and has been described as"the writer's fork.

The lifeline

The life line is an arc around the thumb's base. It begins beneath the first finger and then turns out towards the palm, before returning around the thumb's base.

This line more than any other, is a source of some people to be concerned. When having their palms read. Most of the time, the first question I'm asked is'how long will I live?'. A palm reading can't tell the length of one's life, but a glance at the line of life can frequently reveal the quality of their life.

It is crucial to keep in mind that a lifeline that is short is not a sign of a short life!

A lifeline that is smooth and without scratches or breaks is usually the hallmark of a person who is in overall good health and whose life generally, flows smoothly.

When you take a look at the line of life, you're seeking anything that is that is unusual like breakages, disruptions, an overlap or a crosspoint along the line.

A crossing on this line is a sign of an important issue that has had a negative impact on the person's life. The bigger the cross, the greater the effect of the issue

The lifeline bubble signifies the moment that the person required assistance through a challenging phase.

A clear break can indicate an issue that lasted the duration of break.

Small lines rising up from the lifeline indicate potential for improvement, opportunities and even success.

Lines that connect the life line and the fate line signify the possibility of career or professional potential

The double line of life is a wonderful and lucky mark, the owner of this line can experience many of life's challenges and ups but they'll always come through, they are a survivor.

The process of determining the age at that something happened could be a challenge. For reference for determining the age at which you can see the line at it's longest point, as it curves towards the palm is around 50 years old, so to determine the age of 25 (approximately) you'd be taking a look at a spot in the line that lies between the point at which you begin the line between the age 50 point.

The line of fate.

It is also referred to as"the career line.

The fate line begins low in the palm close to the wrist. It follows the center part of your palm. Its length is variable and could run the full span of the palm and end at the point just beneath your second finger, or only for a few centimeters or stop and begin several times.

The fate line offers information on the career path and the career options It can also show the extent to which a person remains in one particular career path or moves on exploring different opportunities or careers that come along.

A long-running fate line typically is a sign of someone who has been stuck in one thing all their life. It could be an at-home mother or a professional. As you can see, it is not referring to the kind of job the person is in but rather the method they use to achieve it.

If the line is stopped and then starts again, it is likely to be the way in which your life as a worker has been. Beginning and stopping or changing and cutting exploring different career options until they can find one that best fits them.

When the line of fate is located at or above that line of sight, it generally means that the individual decides to pursue the career they want to pursue at a later time in their lives.

If the destiny line begins at or above the heart line , the most suitable career choice for the person could not be identified until after they have reached 50 years old.

If two lines are parallel to one another, the person can be able to pursue two careers or two different paths to life. This is an excellent mark to possess as it makes everything about any profession easier since the owner can endure the most severe of weather conditions that occur.

Minor Lines

The Mercury Line is also known as the Line of Health. The line extends from below the Mercury finger, and then down to the palm , in a straight line. If it is evident, it could indicate a variety of health issues that are usually related to digestion.

It's one of the lines that it's better not to possess! A missing Line of Mercury indicates a healthy general structure.

If there is a line it must be straight and undamaged. If it is broken or bubbles, it may suggest a less-than-healthy structure. The degree of disturbance on the line could indicate the degree of disruption to the health of a person. Often representing digestive problems.

Line of Intuition Line of Intuition

The lines that runs through Mercury as well as the Line of Intuition can be found in the same spot beneath the fingers of Mercury.

The Line of Intuition runs downwards beneath the Mercury finger. It's an arc-shaped line that is located on the right part of the hand below the Mercury finger and lies near or over close to the Mount of the Moon. It is similar to the Mercury line, but it 'bows' outwards into the palm, and ends in the vicinity of the Mount that is the Moon.

If you spot an area that is similar with the Line of Mercury but has an even deeper curve, with one end lying close to the Mount of Mercury while the other is close to the Mount of Moon with a curve that may be as deep into the palm as a third you'll be looking at an intuition line.

The line may be shorter or it can run along the entire length of the palm of your palm.

The person who is in this category is usually a person with an sensitive nature. They may be able to anticipate events before they occur and possess an uncanny understanding of their lives and the choices they need to take.

Like the name suggests, those who have this kind of line will have sharp sense of smell and is most likely to work in the spiritual and psychic realms in some way. They might have regular premonitions, use tarot cards to reading palms, or even be an occult medium.

If you notice this pattern on someone who doesn't work with psychics, they are likely to be doing so at some point later.

It is essential to examine for this line to see if it is visible on both palms, it usually does, but it is likely to be more distinct on one hand than the other.

When the line appears more clear and more refined in the palm that is not dominant, the person is born with the ability to operate within the psychic realm, but they have not yet been able to develop them to their full extent.

When the line appears developed in the dominant palm the owner will likely have developed the abilities they had as a child to a very high standard. likely to be working in the field of spirituality in some way, or possess an intense desire and the ability to be successful in this field.

When the Line of Intuition is visible in both palms the person who is wearing it is likely to be spiritually well-developed and aware.

The Sun line can be found right under the Sun/Apollo fingers. It extends upwards toward the Sun/Apollo finger.it is usually a very short line that is no longer than 2cm/1" in length.

I prefer calling this"the happiness line. The longer the line , the more content the person will be with every aspect of their lives. Even when their life is not perfect and they're facing difficulties this line will reveal its owner to be positive and optimistic.

The line doesn't usually extend further into the palm that the line at head.

The presence of this line suggests that the owner is lucky throughout their life , and even when things don't go well for them, their luck is likely to be able to turn around and bring them an outcome that is positive.

Marriage/relationship lines are found below the finger of Mercury, you will see them as short lines on the very outside edge of the hand. Each tiny line you observe is believed to be a signification of the relationship, marriage or an affair that is heartfelt.

These are not easy lines to understand, as they may have multiple meanings.

Lines on the hands of the non-dominant could indicate potential for relationships and lines on the dominant hand hand are a reflection of relationships that the person has or is likely to have. It is believed that the more deeply embedded into the hand the line appears more deep the relationship will most likely to become. One line doesn't always indicate a single relationship. It could indicate a powerful relationship, or multiple relationships that are equally intense.

A lot of fine lines could indicate that a person is still searching for the perfect partner or they've had several relationships, but weren't certain if they'd found "the one".

If any line ends with a line that is short and blocking it, that signifies that the relationship has ended abruptly.

A small gap in a line of relationship indicates an end to the relationship and duration of break indicates the length of time that the break was for.

If the line ended in a fork, everyone took their own path.

Fine lines that pass through the relationship line indicate issues within the relation.

Some believe that the more line that runs from the base on the fingers of Mercury the older the person was at the time they first met their partner.

Children. Certain palm readers think that tiny lines at the end of the relationship show the number of children that the person has. Some believe that children are identified by the series of islands that are believed to be the basis of the thumb Check out what your research shows and what you think is more exact.

Reading palms is a combination of your perception of what perceive, as well as the intuitive thoughts that you get as you read the palm.

Fertility. Issues with fertility are manifested by weak or unevenly curled racettes (bracelets) They are located on the wrists just below the bottom of your palm. This doesn't necessarily mean that someone will never have children, but could suggest that it could be more challenging and medical assistance or intervention might be required.

Important marks and mounts

When looking at any marks on the palm, it's essential to consider the hand that is not dominant first, and then compare it with your dominant hand (the one that is used to write). Then, you will be able to determine how someone uses and applied the characteristics their parents gave them (shown in the hand that is not dominant) and the characteristics they've acquired (shown on the dominant hand.)

Below each finger, and at the top of the thumb, there is the mount. A mount is a elevated fleshy region. Mounts for four fingers are similar names to the fingers over it. They can also reveal information about the person who owns the hand you're studying.

If the mounts are big and soft, certain characteristics of the mount will be applicable to the owner. A small or flat mount generally diminishes the qualities.

It is the Mount of Venus.

Starting by the mount Venus located on the bottom of your thumb we'll begin to work our way through the other hand's mounts.

While you are looking at your Mount of Venus, check whether it is soft and flat, smooth with a hard surface, or elevated and fleshy. This Mount of Venus represents known as the Mount that symbolizes love and is connected to love of all things including romantic love food, drink thrills and adventures. A huge and delicate Mount of Venus can indicate an excessive desire for food or drinks and an inability to managing their lives and responsibilities, with excessive consumption in every aspect of life leading to a dilemma.

A massive Mount of Venus could also be a sign of the person who is seeking adrenaline and thrills of all kinds and is willing be risky to reach their objectives.

When it is the case that Mount of Venus is soft to the touch, the owner is most likely to be soft and affectionate.

A more firm mount is typically owned by extremely practical people They may appear as aloof or stoic They prefer to keep their feelings private.

A flat and hard Mount of Venus can suggest that the owner is trying to hide their emotions. They may at times appear to "stand offish'.

An Mount of Venus which is balanced and proportional to the hand's rest is the sign of someone who is able to maintain balance in all aspects of their lives.

A lot of fine lines on this wall can signify the sensitive nature of the person and thick horizontal lines indicate solid friendships that the person has had throughout their lifetime.

A large X typically signifies that there will only be one significant love in the lifetime of the person.

If there's any triangles in the Mount of Venus, the owner can marry to achieve the sake of money and success, but not to be in love!

It is the Mount of the Moon

Just opposite directly to Mount of Venus on the outer edge of one's hand lies The Mount of the Moon, it reflects the person's feelings, their imagination and spiritual or religious beliefs as well as their desire to travel.

A massive Mount of the Moon, occasionally with a slight downward bulge, is usually located in the palms of someone who is a follower or student of religious or spiritual practices or who is engaged in an interest in the field of religion or spirituality.

A complete and round Mount of the Moon often is the result of someone with a lot of empathy for other people and a very compassionate nature.

If the wall has deep vertical lines this could indicate the individual's love of traveling and the excitement of learning new things. It is important to examine the entire hand to determine what is the most appropriate for the person.

An X-shaped pattern in the Mount of the Moon can represent someone who is not satisfied with their potential and capability to be successful, and this may be manifested as dominance and the need to manage.

A triangle is a sign of a highly imaginative person. The bigger the triangle, the greater capacity to be creative.

The Mount of Mercury Mount of Mercury

The Mount of Mercury lies beneath the little finger. A huge mount in this case usually belongs to those who are filled with energy and fresh ideas. They are likely to be outstanding communicaters in both spoken and written word.

A single, deeply drawn horizontal line on the Mount of Mercury can be an extremely fortunate sign of winning a lottery or windfall or inheritance arriving to the winner.

The triangle shape belongs to those who are proficient in communicating and can be able to see both sides of an issue in a diplomatic and fair manner.

A person who has a clear star pattern in the center of the Mount of Mercury might struggle to be truthful or even be living in a world of fantasy.

Sun and the Mount

The Mount of Apollo/Sun can be located beneath the ring finger and could reveal some of the traits and dedication capabilities of the person who wears it.

A lot of actor will be sporting a massive Mount of Apollo.

The mount is usually found as a palm someone who enjoys the spotlight and loves using their outstanding communications skills to impress others around them.

A big the X on this wall signifies the success of business, especially when connected to creativity and art.

An equilateral triangle located on the Mount of Apollo indicates that the person who owns this palm will assist others to reach their goals.

Horizontal lines signify the ability to be creative and artistic. If there is the appearance of a square beneath this mount the person who has that hand would have the possibility of promoting and presenting their work for advancement.

The Mount of Saturn Mount of Saturn

The Mount of Saturn lies beneath the middle finger. The mount is often an indication of the academic aspect of an individual. Lecturers or teachers are typically seen with the squares in this type of mount.

A single, long line on this mount indicates the best luck in the course of a person's life when it is exceptionally long, can be believed to signify an end to the life of peace.

A triangle can be located on the hands of someone who has an inner strength as well as an ability to deal with everything that comes their path.

If you notice the uncommon circle on this mount, the owner is guaranteed to have luck throughout their lifetime.

The Mount of Jupiter Mount of Jupiter

On the first finger is beneath the finger lies the Mount of Jupiter, if it is huge in comparison to other mounts in the hand the individual may take life way too seriously. A higher Jupiter mount is typically seen in the hands of actors or people who employ acting skills to advance their careers such as public speakers or lawyers for instance.

A very high Mount of Jupiter is a sign of someone who is in control of their life. They have a positive outlook and are determined to accomplish their goals. They don't like being given a set of rules and should be in control of the direction that their life is taking.

Stars on the mountain of Jupiter is an uncommon and remarkable feature since it shows that the person who owns it is likely to be extremely successful, perhaps even famous.

A X is a sign of the probability of a long, joyful and affectionate relationship.

The triangle shape can signify someone who is able to handle others with compassion and effectiveness manner. This could show in their interactions with their family and friends, or how they handle their work life.

All the the marks on this mount are linked to success and power.

Other marks are also visible in the palm.

The hand should be flat, palm facing up, with your eyes at eye level. Determine which mount is the highest and the largest, it is the one that is most influential on the personality of a person.

If, when you look at your hand, it appears that the Mount of Venus and the Mount of the Moon flow together to form one large region, it is believed to be a sign of a spiritually minded person.

Three X shapes that are found within the main lines on the palm, are believed to signify psychic abilities and the potential.

If the three main lineaments of your palm including the heart line, lifeline and head line be joined at their ends with fine lines, and create the letter M on this palm person who wears it is most likely to enjoy an extremely long and blissful union or romantic relationship.

Chapter 2: Palm Reading Proficiency

The first step towards achieving proficiency with reading the palm when you have an open-minded mindset is to understand the basic principles of the system. Palmists don't just remember all the "rules" and their meanings of the lines, they study it, take on all the variables involved and then work through the palmistry's rules of structure and process before making any predictions.

If you're looking to become proficient at hand reading and a proficient hand reader, you must develop as a hand reader by continuously improving your abilities, and establishing your own style of reading' that is in line with the latest. The same is true for when learning to speak a different language. you need to learn more than the basic concepts of words and the significance behind them and you should also be able to utilize the language in a sentence, knowing how to write and speak according to these rules however, you must be able to alter it according to your own style of writing and speaking style and be able to convey your emotions by using the medium in the way you feel about it and keep in mind the person you're speaking to.

Like any other subject There are many aspects to be considered prior to making any conclusion, claim or, in this instance prediction. The time is crucial as you'll improve in your ability to read palms by attempting it for a certain amount of time, and studying the technique over and over repeatedly. In this chapter, you'll get acquainted with some information and tips to help you becoming an expert palm reader (or at the very least, close to becoming one).

Does the hand really have the ability to predict the future?

Before I give you some advice on how you can become proficient in palm reading there's a problem that has to be addressed first before anyone can truly believe that they be able to recognize the palm of a hand and having an idea of the future of someone.

There are many who question whether or not one could actually master the art of studying palms. The idea of forecasting the future, or getting a glimpse of it is a controversial subject which is debated and debated throughout the history of mankind!

There are some with the belief that the human hand could predict the future. However, obviously many people think it's a ridiculous idea and many aren't even willing to think about the possibility. It's a surprising fact that everyone are able to predict the future! We are actually doing it every day in our lives. One example is when you create an agenda or following a timetable you can predict precisely the events that will occur or what you wish to occur in your schedule with precision this alone is an "fortune teller."

Another example is that in the medical field, doctors are able to identify if their patient suffers from an illness that is fatal or illness, and the length of time it takes to recover, or whether they are heading towards death or. If you consider the matter, there isn't a book or set of rules that tell doctors what to say (about the likelihood that a person is likely to die if they contract the disease in a particular way.). The diagnosis of a doctor is derived on scientific evidence and facts but it's still not definitive, and the circumstances may be changed, and therefore, they are unable to declare the exact timeframe for what is likely to occur and the question is, how do doctors predict their patients' fate with a reasonable level of certainty more often than they do?

The reason is that doctors understand how certain diseases work through experience and decades of knowledge. They are aware of the facts about the causes, the consequences, how the disease progresses and every aspect that must be taken into consideration in addition to the myriad of guidelines and clues that are in form of signs or laboratory tests, and the patient's past. They draw conclusions from these variables and can determine the fate of the patient and determine the probable outcomes through connecting the dots on these factors and the overall structure of science as well as their decades of knowledge. The same is true for palmistry. The main different is that the palmistry deals with the psychology , or the essence that is the brain as well as the individual's personal self.

There is no thing more complex as the brain of a human. there are a lot of questions to answer about the brain's workings However, it seems that scientists are far from knowing the entire truth about it , as it is constantly changing.

According to the experts they believe that the hand is the instrument of the brain, and that is the reason it is the location in which the brain "prints out" its thoughts. In essence, the brain predicts the future direction of a person's existence by collecting all existence and non-existence information as well as the person's environment over a long time. It records everything, makes patterns, and then connects the potential outcomes. It makes a decision from that, and prints its forecasts or expectations to be handed out to.

A majority of people disagree and question the value of palmistry as a predictor because the lines of hands can change occasionally. Hand prints change, but it is not a common event. If it happens, however then it is likely that the person is experiencing changes in their nature that was not thought to be anticipated from the mind. It's a change that is so distinct that no trace of it exists in the life records of the individual. The brain is unable to draw any significant conclusions from it, however the brain is conscious of any change and its response to an incident or a new event. In the process, the brain alters its inputs, which are then refracted by the alteration of lines in the palm.

If you're a student of palmistry it is vital to be aware that predicting the future of your subject by making a mark on his or her hand isn't a guarantee since everything is subject to alter. It's basically just translating what their brains are predicting - you do not make the prediction, it's your brain is the subject's. It's simply reading them, but you must explain the brain's printout is merely something the mind interpreted from past events and, consequently, it may differ from what could be happening in their current or future life. The handprint is only an indication of what the mind thinks about in the near future. However, there's always the possibility that something unexpected could occur that can trigger a changes or modifications in the life of the person who is not anticipated to be anticipated by their brain. Similar to how doctors assess their patients' health or stock brokers anticipate the lows and highs in the markets, palmistry can do similar things and follows the same reasoning based on past events.

Can the hand predict the future? Yes, but not necessarily. Individuals' choices today can affect future events which even the individual's brain cannot anticipate. Keep in mind that the future is not yet written, and is only planned. You can do yourself an favor and be amazed!

How to Improve Your Skills as a Palm Reader

Most people seek clarity or assistance from palmists due to the fact that they're worried about certain issues in their lives, certain important issues in a sense. In most cases, people seek to receive a straightforward"yes or no" answer from their palmists. But, as you've learned so far, it's not so straightforward as you might think and there's no easy solution to the chiromancy. If you're doing research or are doing the practice of reading palms the majority of people pose difficult questions, such as whom they will marry or what they should take in a specific situation that they're in. If you're committed to becoming a professional palmist, don't hurry, and you should remain at the helm of your readings. Don't just look at palms of others in the hope to answer their questions.

There isn't a quick routine for palm reading. As mentioned previously, each person is differentand their conditions are always changing that is why each reading is able to be modified. If your subjects ask you these questions, you shouldn't offer your students a pre given prediction as it may neither benefit you nor your subjects in any way. It will be difficult to defend yourself long-term when your subjects are asked a follow-up question. As the palmist, you must to be aware of the fundamental idea of the key points of palmistry and you need an approach that allows you to study your subject's palms on a rational approach so that you are able to read them objectively.

Like all other things learning is a process that takes time and the most efficient method to improve your skills is to learn things slowly to get faster at this. You'll develop greater precision and depth when you expand your understanding and practice as you progress.

True palmists are never unwilling to acknowledge that chiromancy has its limitations Don't be afraid of asking questions (similar to psychologists or psychiatrists) since through this process you will be able to discover more about the person's previous experiences which will help you better understand the subject matter and increase your ability to comprehend different features and marks in hand prints.

Be aware that palm readers are not supposed to "blind their clients with scientific terms." Based on Benham the famous author of palmistry, he claimed that insecure palmists or dishonest palm readers employ jargons or scientific terms to make their customers be unable to comprehend or not ask further questions of them. The entire purpose behind the palm reader is interpret and read palms in order to assist people to gain an understanding of their own. So, you must be able to communicate your interpretations in a layman's terms; and you must choose the words you use in a manner that allows your reader to understand your interpretations.

If you're hoping to become skilled in reading palms and earn the trust of your clients, you must be able to demonstrate the importance of integrity. This is the primary characteristic that palmists and practitioners must possess from the beginning. It's not just helping to improve your proficiency but also ensure that you are grounded and will not profit from people's ignorance or ignorance. Be careful not to be caught to make a statement to make your clients feel better. Do not be afraid to speak the truth and confess it to your customer/s in the event that you aren't sure of the answer to their questions.

Chapter 3: Cheirology

The Essentials of Palmistry

In this chapter, you'll be introduced to Cheirology which is an investigation of physical characteristics that affect the hands. As was mentioned in the prior chapter that the hands are the "servant of the brain,"" the hands play a role in virtually every activity we engage in in our lives. Before we move on to the fundamentals understanding of reading palms, the student or practitioner must also learn and be familiar with all aspects of the hand as it's in what is known as the "bigger overall picture."

It is essential to know how to handle different aspects because they affect how you read and interpret the meaning behind hand prints.

What exactly is Cheirology?

Cheirology is not much to have to do with the lines found in the palms. However, it is essential to know the hand's anatomy before studying to get an in-depth conclusion and provide an accurate and precise interpretation of the handprints of your subject. Cheirology is the study of the hand (both both right and left) comprising the length of fingers, fingers, its nails as well as the'mounts' in the palm, its shape, color, and even its firmness , or its softness.

The majority of people who attempt to learn about palmistry first time tend to focus only on the hand prints and lines but they do not look at other areas of the hand. This can affect accuracy of readings. In fact, it is an integral part of the study of palms. The study of hands (fingers sizes, lengths, and length, etc.) is essential to understand the character and nature of your client or person.

For some newbies, aspects such as the length of fingers or the size of hands cause a lot confusion. It can be quite difficult to determine if your fingers are medium, long, or short, as well as what type of hand your person has. (Later on , we'll discuss the various types of hands, as well as the meaning and significance of the different sizes, colors and texture, etc.) This is where be able to maintain a sense balance and reliance on your own judgement comes into. Your sense of intuition is acquired over time and consistent use. You can, however, identify fingers and hands correctly in the event that you are balancing everything; one choice will make more sense than the other however make sure you evaluate it carefully to make the right choice. The ability to classify the hand's type or the length/type of fingers correctly is vital since it plays an important an impact on the overall assessment. Only practice and time will help a palmist become proficient in quickly assessing and categorizing the hand correctly.

Next, in the section below you'll get an overview of the various hand parts that are involved and how they aid in understanding the handprint of your subject.

The Hand's Physical Properties

Before we get into the fundamentals of reading palms Here's a quick overview of the various aspects you'll have to take into consideration to aid in reading handprints accurately. In the coming chapters, we'll delve further into the ways these aspects influence the overall meaning of your palm so that you can appreciate the importance and complexity of the specifics.

Skin Texture

The palmistry of skin texture refers to the inherent degree of the hand's refinement. It is possible to determine the skin's texture by looking on the back of their hand. It is essential to identify the skin texture of the person you're studying in order to provide an accurate description.

Palm Color

The palm color can reveal the warmth and vitality that your person.

Hand Consistency

The hand's consistency shows the level of energy of your client. It is possible to determine the "fullness" or "nothingness' of of the person you're studying by feeling their hand, and observing the level of its elasticity or capability for the human body to regain its shape after deforming. If the hand is able to have an elasticity or springiness to it then it's elastic.

Hand Flexibility

This can be difficult to comprehend, especially for newbies. The presence of a flexible hand typically is a sign of the mental flexibility and their ability to adapt to new thoughts and conditions.

Fingers Lengths

The length of a finger typically indicates the level of thought your client will likely to engage on a specific subject or how deeply they will go into a specific topic that catches their interest.

Finger Knots

The knots on the fingers indicate the mental the mind of an individual. It's either a smooth cover type or knotted fingers.

Finger Phalanges

The finger phalanges control the mind of a person as well as the subject matter that he/she is most worried about. It could be their marital situation, their family life or relationships, the work environment, etc.

Fingertip Shapes

The shape of one's fingertip is a good indicator of their mental state.

The Thumb

Thumbs can be classified into various kinds, just like the size of the hand as well as the fingers. Examining the thumb can help the palmist have a clear understanding of the person's personality or personality.

The Mounts

These mounts (which will be covered later within this publication) will allow an expert to discover the most important desires of your subject as well as their passions and their true goals in their lives.

Active and Passive Zones within the Hand

This will allow a palmist to discern if the subject is inclined to create circumstances or let events occur to them.

The Left Hand and the Right Hand

The first thing you must decide before making a palm reading is if the subject is right or left handed. Then, you must take a look at both hands before coming to any judgments or deciding on which hand you'll settle on to read.

The common sense of 2 hands refers to they are the "active hand" or the hand that performs the majority activities is the hand which records the present in contrast,"passive hand" records the past "passive hand" typically records the characteristics the person was born with. Alternatively, if you want to know the person you're born with it is possible to say that this is the baseline of an individual before the brain made assumptions about the individual's future. The majority of people are right handed (active hand) but one hand on the left is passive and for those who are left handed it's the reverse and vice reverse.

However, if this is the case, then the passive hand isn't likely to change because it's something you're born with, and it's better to think of it as the passive hand is a sign of traits and the person's attitude when he or she has laid the foundations for his or her life.

Many psychologists agree that it's in our early years that we begin to build the foundations of our lives that will help us grow older. The choices, decisions made, decisions, and assumptions we make in our early times affect how we become adults. This involves how we relate to other people as well as our own self as well as the way we view the world we live in. These will form the basis of who we'll be, and hence the distinction between the two hands. The passive hand represents the subconscious aspects of our personality when our bodies evolved as we moved through different phases while the active hand represents our inner and conscious aspects of who we are and the way in which we has grown and changed since the point of beginning.

Examining both hands can determine the development and progress of your subject throughout the years, regardless of whether they have developed in an upward or downward direction. If the fingerprints of two hands look similar, it could indicate that someone just kind of swung according to whatever talent or disposition they had after their childhood ended.

If the active hand has more negative prints more than those of the passive hand this indicates that the person was enticed by the numerous temptations that were presented to them, and may have did not make the most of their abilities and talents in the years following their childhood. If the active hand has higher positive marks than the passive it indicates that the person made an efforts to improve the abilities of his/her talent and create something new from the things they began in their early years. Sometimes, this growth occurs due to necessity, but at other times, it's an individual's decision.

Changes in the form of hand prints is rare, but if you happen to encounter something similar it will indicate that significant modifications have occurred by that individual, particularly their unconscious and inner self as well as the foundations was laid in his or her childhood. It is also possible that the person changed the ideas or values that he/she believed in since childhood. It could happen if the person was involved in a painful experience that forced to a change in his/her values and the foundation.

The texture of the skin

The first step to being a professional palm reader, is to determine the condition of your client's skin. In this book the texture will be divided into seven categories that include extremely fine medium, fine medium, fine, coarse, coarse in addition to extremely rough. In order to help novices understand the concept and be able to recognize the texture of palms which they'll encounter. Examining the surface the skin has is vital to understand your subject's character.

In essence, the more refined the texture, the more sophisticated the person. This implies that people with finer skin are more sensitive and their behavior or mood are easily influenced by an event that causes them to be upset. If the person is characterized by rougher and coarser texture on their skin, this usually indicates that the person is more simple, and a simple type of person. These types of people are easy to spot and aren't in any way affected by events which happen to them.

In the next section , you'll get a short and simple review of every skin texture to help you sort out the type of hand the hand you're is reading.

Extremely Fine Skin Texture

Hand texture are uncommon.

Apart from being extremely delicate, it's extremely delicate and soft, which suggests that they are sophisticated , and they can easily be annoyed when something they see is not in line with their sense of self-respect or refinement.

* These individuals like delicate or fine things, and avoid anything harsh or vulgar as it may cause them pain.

Fine Skin Texture

* This is among the most popular skin textures that you'll come across. It's similar to very delicate texture.

These types of people prefer to hang out with similarly sophisticated people.

* They generally respect more low-down - to ordinary people, such as those working employed in entry-level positions or similar positions, but they might not be able to appreciate their group in a social setting.

Medium - Fine Skin Texture

* This indicates that your subject is at peace with their personality, balancing what is down to earth and the more sophisticated or refined.

* Because it's classified as medium-fine this kind of person is still refined in the natural world.

Medium Skin Texture

* These types of palms are not common and not many specialists use this type of classification.

* It's sometimes difficult to recognize, but a the medium texture of skin has an flexibility to it.

* Those with moderate skin textures often find a way to balance sophistication and simple.

Medium - Coarse Skin Texture

The species is easily recognized and may be seen frequently.

* While there's a feeling of coarseness however, it's still not enough to qualify as rough.

* Usually means being balanced and well-balanced, however it can also indicate an affinity for earthiness.

Coarse Skin Texture

It is usually recognized because the hand's skin palm's back is rough and leathery. This suggests a person tends to be straightforward easy to understand and low-key nature

These types of people generally do not care about the intricacies of life and they have a deep dislike of anything they consider to be preposterous.

Very Coarse Skin Texture

* Very uncommon to find, comparable to extremely delicate texture.

It's easy to identify because the skin on the hand's back appears extremely rough and coarse. It looks as if it's made of extremely poor quality leather.

* It's usually encountered on people who live in primitive conditions.

* People who have this type of look are primitive in their basic nature, and are also uninterested in any type of sophistication or anything they think of as pretentious.

* These types of people are so simple, extremely easy to comprehend and do not understand the complexity of modern life; maybe they're also practical.

Hand Consistency

The hand's consistency as well as skin texture the color of the palm and flexibility can assist any practitioner to read their palms more effectively because it provides a wealth of information. According to numerous experts even if you're not equipped with understanding of palmistry, and can only depend on the texture of your skin, its consistency, flexibility and color, you'll still perform precise and thorough readings! This is how crucial these aspects are!

Hand consistency can be determined by taking the hand of your subject and then applying a gentle pressure to determine how flexible the flesh feels. You can try shaking their hand to give you an idea. Also, you should ask your subject to spread out their hand , and then press on the inside of their palm using the thumb's ball to determine how much resistance they have.

Similar to the skin's texture hand consistency can be classified into a variety of types, including extremely hard elastic-hard, hard soft, elastic, elastic extremely soft and flabby.

In the next section , you'll get a short and simple description of every type of hand's consistency, so you are able to easily categorize the hands of your subject.

Very hard-working hands

* Extremely rare and definitely has strong signs

It is virtually inflexible and is difficult to squeeze or press

This usually means that the person is a very active person who is extremely engaged and always willing to take on anything that he/she can be able to do.

* People like these are not intelligent and, often, they're working on some thing without giving it a thought.

Hard Hands

It is often compared to extremely tough hands. It's also noticeable since it's possible to squeeze or press it, but there's no movement to it. But, there's a hint of elasticity

* Nearly has the same traits with extremely tough hands. The one difference might be that they're not as unfocused in the way they invest their energy.

Elastic, Hard Hands

* Is the type of hand with an amount of elasticity that is sufficient to keep its being classified as hard.

The most common way to show you're subject bursting with energy but that it is well directed.

Elastic Hands

It has a particular amount of firmness and can be quite difficult to press. However, once you let it go, your flesh, it bounces as an inflatable ball.

* is usually a sign that the person has an enormous amount of energy, but is also smart in their approach to things.

* They are hard-working and are smart about it; paying attention to the task at hand and don't want to invest their time and energy on things that aren't worthwhile.

* They're also full of life , but they're a perfect balance

The most common is in people who are successful.

Elastic Soft Hands

* Even though the hands are elastic you are able to easily identify or distinguish it as there is a certain amount of softness in the skin. It isn't bouncing back like elastic hands.

It usually means that someone will work long hours to achieve what they desire. They are people who have a feeling of lazyness, however sometimes this is outweighed by their need to be productive.

* It is also a way to demonstrate that the person enjoys working just as they are enjoying other activities.

* They usually seek an occupation that is relaxing but isn't too physically or mentally demanding.

Soft Hands

It is easily identifiable because it's very soft once pressurized and has no elasticity

The word "typically" indicates that the person has a lazy disposition and loves to indulge in certain things over the course of a day.

The person usually has the intelligence and skill, but does not exert any effort.

Very soft and smooth hands.

* These are extreme signs and they are also easily recognized due to the fact that when you squeeze the hand, it appears as if their flesh is leaking out!

* It's also a sign that the person is inactive.

* A dreamer, but not an action-oriented person.

They don't often make an effort to bring their thoughts or desires.

Hand Flexibility

The hand's flexibility shows the flexibility of your subject's mind as well as the capacity to adapt their mindset to new and evolving concepts, innovative methods of doing things and the changing environment.

The general rule of thumb regarding flexibility is the greater flexibility of your hand is, the more flexible the mental attitude. The more rigid the hand is it is, the more rigid and rigid, and less flexible the mind. To determine the level of flexibility, you must place the fingers of your subject in one hand , and then support their wrists with the other , and then apply gentle pressure until you've bent your hand to the extent it can be able to. Be cautious not to injure the person!

Palm Color

The colors of palms can inform an insight into the personality of their subject , whether they're friendly or warm hot-blooded, cannot control their temper, cold-hearted or self-contained. But, other aspects like the temperature in the room and their country of birth is important to consider all of the factors before making any assertions. Colors are further divided into various groups, namely: very red, red pinky-red and pinky white white, and extremely white.

In the next part, you'll be provided with a brief and easy-to-read overview of each color of palm so that you can easily categorize the hand of your subject.

Very Red Color Red Color

* is usually a sign of extreme or a ferocious temper, but can also be quite exaggerated.

It is common for people to not exercise moderately; you're an example, say, a alcoholic It will be difficult to quit.

Red Color

* Often seen in the wild; it also exhibits an intense and intense temper

* When red palmed individuals get into love with one another, they are devoted with all their hearts, however sometimes their passion is a cause to scare their partners away.

Pinky - Red Color

* Red signifies heat, and pink represents warmth. If someone you know has pinky-red palm, it means they're warmer, however they may be more likely to be occasionally intense.

Pink Color

Pink palms are the best color or the perfect color, if your subject is pink-colored, it means that they are is cheerful, warm, and lively in a manner.

They're great friends and radiate just the just the right amount of warmth their personalities.

Pinky White Color

It is also easily identifiable due to the mix of pinking and whitish colors

* usually signifies that someone tends to be warm however they are more likely to be "cool" about certain things.

They are warm and happy, but they can also be prone to be lukewarm.

White Color

* White can be described as having the status of "cold," that means the person does not feel warm and is generally at a distance from the world.

The minds of these people are generally active , but they don't have an intense desire to meet others

The majority of people are selfish and not beneficial in nature.

Extremely White Color

It is extremely rare to come across the same kind of red-colored palm. Sometimes, it appears pale and the palm appears lifeless.

* They have a cold view and attitude to life. highly self-containedto themselves, selfish and completely uncaring.

* If they fall in love with their perfect partner they aren't able to show or display their

feelings, and are generally, they are more idealistic than passionate.

Blue and Yellow Colored Palms

The palms with yellow hues typically indicate an uneasy personality. It is also a sign of a pessimistic outlook On the other hand the blue color of palms generally suggest a slow flow of blood and, often, an insufficiency of the heart (both physically as well as emotionally).

Different types of Fingers, Palms, and Mount

In order to gain understanding of the real nature of the person you're studying it is important to look at factors like the form of the palms, the size and shape of fingers, the fingertips and fingers, the nails and the mounts prior to being able to begin reading the lines. By doing this, you will be able to get better accuracy in reading and also improve the ability of an expert palmist. Once you've mastered these fundamentals and techniques, you'll be able read more easily and with more confidence.

Finger Length

In addition to other aspects such as the texture of the skin hand texture, hand flexibility, hand consistency and the color of the palm The next thing to determine will be the size of fingers. The length of the fingers will provide an idea of the level of your subject's mind. In the next part, you'll be provided with a short and easy-to-read list of the various lengths of fingers to help you classify the hand of your subject.

Very Long Fingers

As with other extremes, long finger types aren't often discovered.

* This type of person is a hyper-developed person, or those who is constantly thinking about everything.

* People like these are typically so engaged in their field of study that not a single aspect is left unnoticed.

* They can fail to see the "bigger image."

Long Fingers

* Very frequent

* usually suggests that the individual thinks very deeply about anything that catches their interest.

They are extremely sensitive and are also susceptible to be suspicious of people around them.

Medium - Long Fingers

* It's quite length, but it isn't enough to qualify as having long fingers.

* Most often indicates a healthy equilibrium between a need to think about issues while paying attention small details and also a desire to accomplish things.

Medium Fingers

The term "balance" usually indicates a mental attitude

* People who pay enough attention what they're focusing on, but nothing more than.

* They handle all the details that are required and then focus on getting the job done.

Medium - Short Fingers

* Also indicates that the person is at ease in using their mind.

Most people want to have a broad view of the world and ignore the details they think are not important.

Short Fingers

* is usually a sign of someone who isn't a fan of dealing with irrelevant details.

A lot times those who are like this simply want to make their point clear.

* They're quick in making decisions. This is due to the fact the fact that they organize things on a massive size, which could be problematic sometimes because they tend to miss important aspects that could cause issues.

Very Short Fingers

This usually means that the person is also not comfortable being thinking about something that isn't their own (this kind of person shouldn't be employed in jobs like event management or something similar).

Additionally, they are driven by their feelings and is driven to finish things quickly.

Fingertips: Different Types

The shape of fingers symbolize the mind of your subject and its fingers represent the mental outlook of your subject. In this section, you'll provided with a simple and quick way to learn about the significance and meanings of the various fingertips of six different types, namely spatulate, square conic, rounded and psychic.

Spatulate Fingers

If the fingers of your patient are flaring out or wide in the tips similar to spatulas used by chemists, you could classify it as a spatula finger.

* Usually means that your subject is extremely active and is not willing to conform or to accept the world as it are.

* People like these are always seeking something different or new. They're the type of people who don't adhere to the norms of society; simply because everyone else is doing things in a certain manner there is no reason to think that they shouldn't follow the same.

The majority of them are types of adventurers of people, such as explorers, trail blazers and explorers within the industry. They are always looking to be different, innovative and are always willing"breaking the rules. "break rule-breaking."

* Someone who is highly creative and has plenty of drive to do something.

Square Fingers

* You will be able to recognize it easily if your fingertips have a square designed.

* usually signifies that the individual is punctual, reliable and organized in their work.

* Very conservative in the manner that they adhere to the same routine or schedule.

* The people mentioned above aren't averse to breaking out of tradition or the established order.

Conic Fingers

* Also known and recognized Fingers from bottom to tip create the appearance of a cone , hence the name.

* Usually means that the person you are talking to is emotionally unstable, impulsive, or unrealistic and easily influenced by their mood.

Their mindset is both open and practical and they feel the task of doing things in a systematic manner is tedious.

• Idealistic in their perspective They live for the moment, enjoy others people, and simply desire to live life to the fullest.

* These types of people possess an artistic nature (where aesthetics are more significant than pragmatics) However, since they aren't regular, they can't often achieve many things.

Round Fingers

* Very popular and is a mix of conic and square shapes.

* It indicates that the subject is practical in their perspective, and is not shackled to a strict order and consistency.

A slight rounding of tips suggests that their practical view is sometimes clouded by intuition and idealism.

Psychotic or Pointed or Pointed Tip Fingers

It is extremely rare to come across The fingers are long and pointed. They are shaped as a conic-shaped finger.

* The pointyness is usually a sign the person has an incredible amount of inspiration, optimism as well as a highly realistic or unrealistic view of life.

* As fingers are long it indicates that the mind dominates, however it is usually a an apprehensive feeling. They tend to be suspicious and skeptical of people around them and can be easily offended.

Philosophic Fingers

* This type of finger is made up with long, pointed fingers with knotty joint.

* The fingers that are long indicate the development of the mind The pointed tips indicate an idealistic view, while knots indicate that the individual tends to analyze every aspect.

The majority of people who have this shape of finger love reasoning and are analytical. Sometimes , they're also optimistic, especially with regards to subjects like theology, philosophy, and the meaning of life.

* Has the habit of looking at their ideas and motivations.

Different kinds of Finger Knots

101

Finger knots come in two varieties either knotted or smooth and you can identify it by looking at how well developed the joint between knuckles of a person.

Fingers with Knotty Fingers

Fingers that are knotty suggest that someone has an extremely strong or a stifling mental realm. It typically means that the person you are talking to is focused meticulous, attentive, thinks about their every move, and are also organized in their daily life.

They're the people who analyze an issue before deciding to accept anything. They need to analyze the issue and look at the issue from a variety of points of view before settling or gaining their agreement on some thing. They are looking to discover the facts and get to the core of any issue and don't like being rush, but once they've settled about something, they'll not change their mind.

Top joints can be known as"knots of mental order. "knots that regulate mental thought." If your subject's joints are developing, it signifies that he or she is inclined to analyze all things mentally based. They do not take things for granted, and they study every aspect, and viewpoint. They record it in their meticulous and well-organized brain.

The middle joints are often referred to as "knots of order in the material world," if your subject's joints are healthy this means that the person prefers to organize the elements of their life. In their house and office, everything will be tidy organized, neat and arranged in a location that is easily accessible.

Smooth Fingers

The smoothness of your fingers indicates that your subject is one who thinks quickly and easily. Like we said earlier, knotty hands suggest how the brain is stifled because it is constantly analyzing Smooth fingers indicate that the mind doesn't slow down to think about everything, and that is the reason they make their decisions on things quickly. The people with smooth fingers are extremely artistic they love beauty and are also spontaneous in their character. They think quickly and frequently make decisions on the basis of impulse or intuition, something that a knotty-fingered person wouldn't do. They are those who take lots of things for granted since they believe it will make their work day quicker and more easily.

The fingers of smooth hands also form knots. And even when your client provides reasons (because of work, sport, or work, etc.) regarding the reason why their hands are knotted the knots only appear as the consequence of mental alteration within the person.

As people get older or more mature and mature, they acquire a more critical outlook and this is the reason why fingers get more advanced or knotty. However, even though this is an issue but it doesn't mean people with smooth fingers aren't able to analyze things. The different is that they look at things they believe are significant, whereas knotty fingered individuals tend to be overthinking everything that is the subject.

Different types of Finger Phalanges

The fingers are a representation of the brain, then the fingers' phalanges symbolize the world inside the mind. These are the physical practical , and mental.

If the phalanges at the bottom of every finger that you are observing lengthy it means that their mind is dominated by things which are related to their personal and physical self. When they are thinking about things they consider their homes, their pleasures and personal comforts.

When the middle phalanges are longer this means that the mind is focused on issues of a practical nature that generally relate to the external globe in some manner.

If your top phalanges have the longest length, this means that the subject's thoughts are very caught by things of an intellectual nature.

For reading , finger phalanges will only be accurate if there are clear distinctions in their lengths. If one phalanx is marginally more developed than the other it is a sign that the brain is not much more likely to focus on the features identified by the larger or larger phalanx.

If the phalanges on the bottom aren't just long and fat, but also fatty and full of puffiness, then your subject is someone who is sexually indulgent because their mind is often occupied with issues concerning their physical and personal pleasure.

If the phalanges at the bottom are narrow and long, this means your subjects are selective with the food they eat as well as the kind of indulgences they'll want to take pleasure in.

Types of Nails

If you notice that your subject has the appearance of a narrow and long nail, it suggests that he/she is a dreamer or idealist by nature. This also indicates that they lack strength and you won't observe them performing heavy manual work, taking part in endurance sports or undertaking activities which require effort. Nails that are broad however, indicate strong body.

Short nails tend to be large and show an impressive structure. They're the kind of person who tend to be argumentative and a bit of a fault-picker.

If the nail of your subject is short and broad, that means they're extremely critical. They're the type of people who even if they know they're in error but they're willing to argue just for reasons of argument.

Nail Color

Pink is always an excellent sign as it signifies good health. Blue indicates a slowing of circulation that could be caused by weakening the heart. Likewise, the purple nail indicates the possibility of some type of heart trouble is possible to be present, particularly in the case of patches of blue on the palm. Nails with tiny white spots suggest it is because the nerve system in a state of stress.

Fluted Nails

Nails that are fluttered usually signify an anxious or nervous state. The more fluting, the more level of tension, and, in a more severe situation the nails turn fragile and white. A nail that is extremely fluted curves downwards to protect the fingers' tips. It also can be curving upwards in an arch. This is a sign of extreme severity of nervous disorder and may affects people who have had a stroke recently or a different type of neurological illness.

Palms: Different Types

There are three distinct types of palms : spatulate palms, square palms, and conic palms. Other books may offer more categories, but it is all categorized into the three main categories. In the next chapter, you'll be provided with a brief and simple overview of the different forms of the palm. This way you can quickly classify your hand's shape and gain a better understanding.

Square Palms

If your subject's is a square-shaped person typically, this means they're practical in the nature of things. Even if you observe a conic hand that shows their idealistic an impulsive mental outlook They are very much a realistic person.

* If you see an oddly rectangular-shaped palm (which is classified as square) this means their physical world is not developing.

Spatulate Palms

* Most likely signifies that your subject's nature is unique and prone to be unique.

* If it's larger at the base the mounts will be original and unique in the world of ideas due to the built Mount of Luna which shows imagination and creativity. (more on mounts to come)

When the palms are larger on top indicates that they are unique and different in all practical aspects.

Conic Palms

* is usually a sign that someone is optimistic and emotional.

Conic palms typically have a larger base that suggests they are fully built and indicates a desire to enjoy the physical.

If your patient is a conic hand but has a fine texture on the skin (refer to the section on skin texture) This indicates that they're refined in their ability to perform physical things.

The Thumb

Authors, palmists, and the founders of modern palmistry are of the opinion that the thumb, though a component of fingers is extremely essential to understand the subject matter because it is unique to an individual. In addition to what you've discovered, other features of your hands like the shape of the palm, the fingertips and lengths of fingers, and so on. can give you a better idea about the character of your subject in nature, personality and attitude regarding their mindset. The thumbs-up as that which experts recommend will provide you with an understanding into the character of the individual or their determination. I'm sure you've heard of the assertion that one may have the best talents that they have, however, if they don't have the character of their creator, then those talents are useless to them.

Willpower, or character, is among the traits that differentiate people from one another. It's a power that even the greatest of powers cannot predict due to its instinctual nature and driven. Character is, in essence, an individual choice. It's not something you're born with it, but you grow your character as age. You make decisions in accordance with your beliefs in your rational thinking, your values, or other elements. Anyone can alter their personality or develop willpower, if they decide to.

The thumb in palmistry is divided in three parts The natural nature, feelings, and the desires. The middle or second phalanx symbolizes the ability of logic and reason , while the top or first one is the phalanx that represents the will or action. The desire to do something (palm) is processed by logic and reason (second the phalanx) before being transformed into action and real (top the phalanx).

The Mounts

Seven mounts are that can be found on the hand, namely: Mount of Jupiter, Saturn, Apollo, Mercury, Moon, Venus along with the Mount of Mars. Each one of them represents the specific aspect of the subject's character. The task for the reader's palm is assess the strength and relative importance of each mount, select the most dominant or strongest zone, and then place other mounts according to their position of prominence. This section will get acquainted with a few basic explanations of each mount.

It is also suggested that you look over the area of each mount so that you will know where it is in your palm.

Mount of Jupiter

Four fingers are present beneath each one of them is an inscription. The first, or thumb lies that the Mount of Jupiter which indicates the desire of the individual to have the control of their life and the people who impact it. If the Mount of Jupiter is prominent , it signifies that the subject has the qualities of a leader. It's a sign that the individual is sincere and optimistic. If it's flat, that indicates that the person has a lack of confidence. If the mount is over it means that the person is over-developed (or truly dominant over other people) it's a sign that the individual is arrogant and arrogant.

Mount of Saturn

The port of Saturn is situated under the second finger or middle finger. It signifies a need for security and stability. It also indicates it indicates that the individual is responsible and is seeking wisdom. If the finger is flat, the individual might be optimistic and enjoys to be social. If, however, it's too swollen and your subject has an extended finger could indicate that they are introverts or is a bit distant from people.

Mount of Apollo

It's situated under the third finger, also known as the rings finger. It usually signifies the desire to display your individuality or distinctiveness. If the ring is well developed, the individual is very positive and warm. However, if it's flat, it typically means that the person is unreliable and cold.

Mount of Mercury

It's located below the fourth finger or the tiny finger and is usually a sign of the desire to be in touch. This is the kind of people who love traveling and is an avid runner. But, if the Mount of Mercury is a bit overdeveloped, that means the person is lying. Flat mounts indicate that the person is boring and shy.

Mount of Moon or Mount of Luna

The bottom of the palm, over the thumb, if it's well-developed, it is usually a sign that the person is caring creative, loving and passionate about life. However, if it's flat, it suggests an empathy level and also a good imagination.

Mount of Venus

They can be seen beneath the thumb, and typically indicates the level of warmth and generosity. If the thumb is well developed, they have a fascinating person to have around them and lives a social life. If the Mount of Venus is not developed, it indicates that the person is greedy and seeks to buy things that are material and if it's flat, it means the person you are talking to lacks passion, and also is selfish.

Mount of Mars

It is the Mount of Mars which is divided into two zones, active and passive. Under that is the Mount of Jupiter and inside the Life Line is the Mount of Lower Mars which signifies the desire of the individual to push or push their way ahead in their life. On the other hand, there is that of the Mount of Upper Mars which is a sign of their determination to adhere to their goals and persevere in their efforts.

In the following chapters, we'll go more deeply into the primary types of lines that are found in the palm, its signs, meaning and the proper reading.

Chapter 4: "The Line Of Heart" Line Of Heart
The heart line is about the person's emotional character as well as its character. In the event that the line seems straight and long, this signifies the subject of your question is guided by their affection and love for their friends, family relatives, as well as the world generally. The more streamlined your line is, the more affected by their connections with other people. They are less inclined to be concerned for their own or be attentive to the needs and desires requirements of those closest to them.

The majority of people seek out a palmist in order to find out things about love life such as when they plan to be married and what kind of partner they will be in relationships with or if it will last or not. It's not that simple, professional palmists tend to limit themselves to this issue to keep from confusion. They tend to focus on signs from the heartline which is related to their relationships generally and not just their romantic relationships.

The Line's Length Line

Excessively Long Line

If the heart of your loved one extends all the way to the palms, it's considered as excessively long. it typically indicates an emotional character. They are controlled with love, and love for their loved ones, however they constantly seek to be surrounded by the love of others. They are extremely possessive and possessive, which can be a problem since they tend to be extremely jealous.

Long Line

If the line of the heart begins in the middle of Mount Jupiter It can be classified as a long line. The meaning is similar to people who have an overly long heart line. They are also ruled by the love of their life. They are loving and affectionate, but they also want much in return. They could be extremely hurt when they're not appreciated.

Short Line

If the line of the heart begins at the mount of Saturn it is considered to be a short line. People with this type of line have a tendency to admire nature and seek an ally, but they are more interested in their personal needs. According to a variety of experts, people with the short length of their heart lines are sensual , but they aren't driven by love or compassion. they're motivated mostly by the desire to be sexually attractive and the desire for a partner or a friend.

Very Short Line

If the heart line starts at the top of Apollo it's considered to be an extremely short length of a heart line. It is usually a sign that the person is cold in their emotions and doesn't take care of the well-being of others. They tend to have unselfish relationships or the type of relationships that serve the interests of their own. If they offer something to which they'd like to receive something back It isn't because they give something to show love or compassion They do it due to their own motives.

General Information on the Heart Line

A straight line from beginning to end means that an individual is consistent in their emotional state and will enjoy a satisfying emotional life.

Wide and thin lines indicate that the person's love life is superficial and unsincere and their life isn't meaningful or satisfying.

A thin line that is in contrast to other lines is an indication of an emotionally self-centered person or one with a self-centered character.

A heart-shaped island line can indicate the signs of instability or unsettlingness, and may be experiencing emotional difficulties. Your loved one may be suffering from split feelings.

The chained the heart line (series of islets) within the palm may display prolonged periods of unsettling and emotional tenseness.

A break in the line can reveal a drastic change in the subject's attitude towards life. This can be caused through being disappointed or depressed by someone they love.

The hollow or dot in the line can have a negative significance as it signifies an intense and sudden period of emotional turmoil.

The little lines that run along the heart are positive and typically signify friendships or affections that are likely to be present in their lives, or feel it.

Split lines that disappear in the direction of the heart lines are considered to be negative and are usually a sign of depressions of the emotional kind. If you see the split line this means that the emotional strain can last the duration of time it runs beneath the line of your heart.

A heart line that is confused or jumbled confusing characters of the line indicate that an individual's emotional state could also be confused or going through an emotional rollercoaster.

Red Line

If the heart line appears colored red this signifies an rise in the intensity of the individual's emotional condition and also the strength and relative force that the heart line has.

Pink Line

This is a sign of an open and caring person, in particular toward their loved ones.

White Line

Similar to the palm color The white line on the heart indicates coldness. When the heart line appears extremely long, the person tends to be in a sense, and will not display compassion.

The Active as well as Passive hand

* If the line of the heart is clearer and more long in the active hand of your subject is a sign they have become more compassionate, loving and selfless person through the years.

* If the line of the heart is clearer and more long in the passive hand of your subject, it typically indicates that he or she has had an incident that led to him/her becoming less affectionate and less likely to give in their personal lives.

Timing of Events

Timing of the events that affect the line of the heart could be a challenge. Indeed, many experienced palmists still debate which point they should base their beginning point for determining the date of readings. For modernist palmists divided lines constitute the ideal starting point to achieve the same coherence, consistency, and simplicity. However, many traditionalists do not agree with this notion, and believe that the ideal starting point should be on the Mount of Jupiter. The form of the line that is under

Jupiter is different from hand to hand and, as we've mentioned previously, it was in the early years of life that the foundation was laid in stone, this is why the Mount of Jupiter is considered to be the best place to start in this particular line.

According to numerous palmists, it's possible to determine the date of events with lines that are precise and consistent by taking a measurement of the line and dividing its length into seventy (to calculate the space that is used by one year) to get satisfactory results, especially with regard to the subject's previous actions. The curvature of the line can make it difficult to determine, however it is possible to use a straightforward method.

You can set a pair of dividers with the distance of one centimeter and then take a measurement of the heart line from beginning to end. After you've determined the length of it, you can adjust the dividers to 10 years intervals (normally 0.9 to 1.2 centimeters) and then work your way across the heart using intuition and understanding to determine the precise year of any markings or modifications to the form that the lines. But the emotional characteristics of people are complex , which is why an in-depth analysis of the past and future is very difficult and only significant prints are considered.

So , if you decide to try this kind of technique or any other approach in general you must be extremely cautious and careful in attempting to forecast the future for your customers or your subjects.

Chapter 5: Line Of Head

The Head Line identifies the subject's mental energy and their ability to rationalize. It also shows the broadness of their thinking, the way they think, as well as the kind of choices they have to make. The Head Line, as per experts, indicates a person's level of intelligence, however nothing could be further from the truth.

Although clear, long and well-formed lines on the head are typically seen on the hands of extremely intelligent people however, they can also be observed on the hands of non-intelligent people! The level of intelligence of a person can be determined by the physical characteristics of their hand, specifically the middle of their thumb. The head line is only pointing at a person's capacity to put their brainpower to work by responding to what they think about when they formulate plans or make decisions on something and take action on their decisions. In this section, we'll examine the various aspects that you need to think about in order to be able to read your palm. We'll talk about the significance and the indications of the length of the head line and also some general guidelines.

The Line's Length Line

The more extensive the line of sight is the bigger the dimension of your subject's thoughts and how much they're influenced by the things they believe. The more narrow the line, is the less extensive their mind as well as the lesser their daily life is influenced or controlled by their thoughts. Here's an indication of each length of the line that runs through their head:

Excessively Long Line

It extends across the hand and reveals the person who is controlled by their mind. They try to rationalize every aspect of their lives according in accordance with what they believe. But, this can also mean that they limit themselves to the issues that their mind can handle with, and anything that is outside the reach of their mind is either ignored or blocked out. People like this are highly analytical and rational They are not able to handle the stress, and if they can't escape, they may experience a mental breakdown.

with long lines that are too long, but they aren't as restricted by their mentality. They can make the most of their mental faculties but they also tend to become too rational with their decisions and attitude to life.

Medium Line

A headline of medium length indicates that your subject's rational mind is well developed. They can make the most of their mental faculties however they are not restricted by the requirement to be rational or highly sighted in all that they undertake or think about. They have control over their minds, however there isn't any doubt about having too much control over their minds or that their lives are constrained by the desire to justify every single thing.

Short Line

A headline that is too short suggests that someone is not in control over their lives. The mind isn't able to fully make use of the intelligence available and they are impulsive in their choices Also, they aren't long-term planners.

Very Short Line

This is merely a sign that the subject has a restricted mental capacity. Therefore, if you see any evidence of intelligence in other areas of their lives the majority of the time it's only a little value. People like this are not able to make long-term decisions due to their one mind that is one track. They may be experts in one area, however they have no knowledge of any other subject, not even their own personal aspects.

General Information regarding the Head Line

A line that is clearly and well-defined across its length indicates that your subject is clear of thought, a consistent goal, a good memory and the ability to manage their self.

A wide and a shallow line is a sign of mental inertia. It's the kind of person who lets themselves drift across the world without a obvious direction. These are known as those who "go along with life" kind of person.

A thin line indicates that they're not able to handle any mental stress or stress from life's situations.

An island is a sign of mental unstable. The person is unable to organize their thoughtsand might be very inconsistent with their choices. If you observe imperfections on the head line you should also take into consideration the quality of the Mount of Luna as defects in this area along the neck line. Lines can be more dangerous when the Moon's Mount is strong, this will indicate whether or not your subject will recover completely.

A chain that is visible in the subject's palm indicates a time of time during which the mind is agitated, or unbalanced.

An unintentional line that begins at the top of Jupiter and connects to the head line a bit down the hand reveals the period when the person was extremely ambitious in their thinking.

Split Lines

Split lines that depart from the head line and follow through the chained head line towards the upwards direction display the time when a person is trying to gain more emotional control over their life.

Split lines that are located in the line of heart and then merges to the brain line indicates that a difficult decision has been taken for the head, and not the heart.

The split lines that hang from the head line display the pull power of imagination on the subject's mindset. People dream and hope but since the head line is still on its planned path, their desires or goals are not fulfilled most of the time.

The Active as well as Passive hand

* If the head line of the active hand is better print than that of the passive hand, that typically signifies that your subject has learned to make more effective use of their mind and is a more rational person and is better at executing their choices.

* People with an elongated headline on their hands active usually has financial issues, the palmist can advise them to be more pragmatic and realistic in order that they can manage their financial situation. However people with a head line that slopes downwards within their hand do not face any issues in their financial situation. Money isn't a problem for them because they are able to

let themselves think more creatively and dream up ideas.

Timing of Events

The dating process in the head line is also very difficult for a lot of experts. It is possible to have a certain amount of success with lines that are well-defined and clear from beginning to end however , it might not be 100% accurate.

One of the major reasons why palmists as well as modernists can't create guidelines that they can count on is the fact that people experience shifts in the way they think and think without conscious awareness how they're changing.

There is a significant delay between when individuals begin to change their thinking and when they realize that they have made changes. Because there are many details and variables that must be considered, establishing a clear and reliable method for determining the date of occasions will need to wait until a fully-equipped research team made up of palmists and experts can come up with a solution and prove the method. Similar to the method employed in the line of the heart in the line of heart, its length is seventy years. And by dividing the length by seventy, the palmist or practitioner could be able determine the amount of distance covered every year.

Chapter 6: Life's Line Of Life

The life line is a representation of elements of physicality in one's physical appearance, however it isn't without nuances in the process that's why it's crucial to take into consideration other aspects before making the final decision or making a prediction. The life line can also reveal the strength of your subject's health and physical strength. It also indicates the impact of these things on the type of life they live, their quality and whether they're likely to have children.

In this section, we'll discuss the various factors you need that you should consider in order to be able to read your palm accurately. We'll talk about the significance and the indications for the existence line, as well as its connection to the active as well as passive hand, as and some general details.

General Characteristics

The life line begins from the palm side in between the mounts Jupiter as well as lower Mars The line then is curved around the Mount of Venus and is finished in the wrist. The higher the length of the line, the greater the time span during which a person can expect to live a healthy life until the end of their life and the smaller the line, the shorter the time they are able to rely on their physical health or may be relying on someone else to look after their needs. It is possible to encounter a hand which isn't a life line however, while this is extremely uncommon, there are certain people who do not have it. If it is, it suggests that the person is lacking vitality, physical strength and is prone to getting sick quickly, and is usually able to survive solely on their nerve energy.

While the length of the line indicates the quality of life and longevity of an individual however, it does not necessarily indicate that one is more likely to live longer if they have a longer length. It also does not mean that people with a shorter lifeline may die at earlier age or suffer in physical strength.

General Information on Life Line

The quality and clarity of the line is crucial to observe. A clear and deep line means that your subject is full of physical strength and has an exciting and fulfilling life.

A deep and wide line signifies a lack of vitality. Even though people do things they love or find pleasure in, they may not feel fulfilled in their lives.

A thin line of life indicates those who are unable to endure tough situation or who is easily exhausted when they attempt to work hard physically for some activity.

If the line goes through minor changes in direction it is a sign of the change in the living habits. If it suddenly begins to follow a larger outward curve , then it indicates that the life style is becoming more vigorous. If it suddenly starts to curve towards the crest of Venus it is a sign that the lifestyle is becoming less active and less confined.

If you notice a crack in the line of life, it is a sign of something serious, and it could also signal a break in the flow of energy within the body. While it is often caused by an accident or illness however, this isn't always the case since a break may be the result of an entire change in the way of life of a person.

A dots on the line generally is a sign of your subject's health. The dots signify an disruption in your subject's energy flow. The greater or more evidently it's marked in the greater the severity of the sign.

An island signifies a separation of energy and an era of struggle in the course of life. The person is uneasy and even though an island typically is a result of a flaw, such as dots, it often suggests that the person is exhausted and inability to to make their life more organized.

A chained line demonstrates long periods of trouble that could affect the health of the individual or their personal wellbeing.

A line of ladders in the life line is a sign of the weakening of your physical body. Your person is not as energetic and is advised to stay clear of stress-related situations. Their levels of energy are typically fluctuating and they can become exhausted. A lot of people who have weak thin, thin, or laddered life paths also have trouble in finding the perfect partner.

Energy Lines

The energy lines may break off from the life line, and move towards an energy lines that rise to the mountain of Jupiter. They are always interesting to observe because they signal that someone is making significant efforts to make improvements or reach a target.

If your palm displays an energy line with a soft consistent, it generally suggests that the person is trying to get over their insanity and also puts in the effort to accomplish their targets.

In the event that one of your lines of energy increases to Jupiter it means that the individual is determined to improve to the top and elevate their standing in the world.

If the line of energy rises to Saturn it is usually a sign that they put in a significant effort to enhance their financial security, status as well as their material health.

Relationship between Palm Colors in Life Line

As was discussed in the previous chapters, the color of the skin is vital to consider as it can either alter or increase the severity of the disease.

A pinkish shade of the line decreases the impact of any flaws within it (such as breaks, dots ladders, dots, etc.). A life line that is reddish is also a positive sign since it enhances the level in the strength of physical energy. If you notice a whitish line, it is a sign of physical fatigue, regardless of whether the line is thick or clearly marked.

The Active as well as Passive hand

* If the line of life on the palm of your active hand isn't so well-defined as the passive hand, then the individual hasn't taken care of their health. The system of the person is affected and as a professional you must advise your client or subject to be more attentive to their health and wellbeing.

* If the line of life is visible on the hand that is active it means that the physical side of

their hand is stronger and more immune to illnesses.

Timing of Events

The timing of events in the life line is comparable to the time of events along the line of the head and heart. However, instead of measuring the duration of the line you must measure the typical distance it's expected to travel.

You could try small separators of one centimeter. The line should be measured starting from its beginning point at the mounting of Venus all the way until the wrist. If it does not end earlier, should simply follow it. The distance from the beginning of your wrist will cover around seventy years in the course of his life. when you set the dividers to 10 year intervals, you can measure the time period through the line, one decade at each decade.

Chapter 7: The Line Of Fate

The line of destiny, often referred to in the form of Saturn Line, also known as Saturn Line indicates the directional behavior of the subject and how it can be affected by different circumstances. The presence of the Fate Line indicates that someone is on the right track in life and is striving to achieve his/her goals and goals, however, should it be poorly marked or damaged (has breaks, splits dots, breaks, and so on.) In any manner, this means that they're having difficulties and are not making the progress they would wish to achieve.

It is a important line since it is connected to the purpose of one's life and the things they have done to accomplish their goals. If the line drawn by destiny is clearly and well-marked, it means they are satisfied in their work and feel they are making progress in their life. If you happen to see an arm that isn't marked with an arrow of fate indicates that your subject has no direction in life , and they just seem to exist , not vice versa.

In this section, we'll examine the various aspects to take into consideration to correctly read a palm. We will discuss the significance and the indications of the fate line and its relationship to the active and passive hand, as well as general details.

General Information regarding the Fate Line

If the line of fate is well-defined and well-marked, it suggests that their job or career is progressing and they feel that they are progressing.

If the line is wide and shallow , it means that your subject is struggling to locate an "break" or the right chance and are dissatisfied with the current trend in life.

A flaw in the line could indicate problems in the profession or the direction of life.

A small island in the fate line is a sign of an era of extreme difficulties and indicates that the individual is agitated and uneasy in that specific time, however chains indicate the length of time that has been characterized by trouble.

The sections of the line that are particularly deep exhibit times of intense struggles and strains in the profession or life direction.

Dots in the line is usually a sign of an abrupt or unexpected difficulties. The state of the line following the dot will indicate the extent to which it affected the course or direction of the person.

A branch line, or offshoot that originates away from the path of destiny and is heading toward to the Mount of Apollo shows the person's perception of success has been greatly improved, however, the type of success they achieve is largely on the individual's perception of values. If the line is rising towards Jupiter this indicates an rise in authority or status and also an increased capacity to affect others, and to control things. The branch lines indicate a brief period of greater success, however when they're long and ascend to the top, this means that the period of increasing performance will last a long time!

A thin line connecting the lines of fate shows the individual's direction of thought was influenced by a different person.

A line of influence that is unable to connect to the fate line, but appears alongside it indicates that the influence has given immense assistance to an individual's career the direction of life.

It is typical to see an unreliable fate Line that gets clearer and stronger after joining the influence line. This can be an indication of marriage and shows that the union has given the individual a real sense of motivation and a sense of direction in their lives.

The fate line gets smaller or more brittle and it runs across the head line, it means that after an age, the individual started to lose desire to maintain their current direction in life or working towards the pursuit of a particular goal.

A deeply-marked, well-marked fate line that runs directly towards Mount of Saturn. Mount of Saturn and is not influenced by any other lines suggests that a person is a person who is very isolated in their lives, and their job or job is what matters to them. They are so focused on what they're doing and where they would like to go, that they forget other aspects that are equally important to life, such as relationships, family, spiritual motives, etc. Anything that hinders their path or slows their progress is likely to be avoided in the subconscious, which includes the marriage process and friends. If your subject does marry, the marriage will not be as important to their professional goals. If there is conflict, their career and personal interests will prevail.

Grills on Saturn is a sign of trouble even when the path to destiny is clearly defined and well-marked. In this case, the person is able to find an idea of what they want to achieve in their lives but they won't achieve what they would like, and may be slow in their development.

If you notice a hollow in the middle of the hand, it is usually something negative about objects of the material world. The hollow is caused by a weak plain of Mars which suggests that the person does not prefer to confront situations like this. If they fail to speak up when they ought to, more difficult situation could arise and make it more difficult to succeed in their lives.

Crossbar Lines

A crossbar is a negative symbol and is a sign of interference with the natural course of the universe.

If it's followed by thinning or weakening of the line, it means the line is causing the person to lose energy and motivation to maintain their course. It is not uncommon to observe a crossbar accompanied by a weakening line that is followed by an abrupt break. In such a situation, it indicates that the interfering has resulted in a loss of enthusiasm and energy in your life. This will be followed by the temporary change in direction.

In the event that the lines are positioned differently, the shift could that could lead to a change in the job or career.

Breaking Lines

A break can be a serious problem. If the direction of your subject ceases to move and then begins again for after a brief period, it signifies that the subject has lost his or her direction over a certain amount of time

If the new line is placed in a different position on hand, or is placed to a completely different angle, it is a complete shift in the overall direction of the person.

If the breaking lines intersect with other lines, this indicates the gradual shift in the direction of a person's life.

If there's no overlap of lines, then the shift is unexpected and may be unintentional.

When you're faced with a break in the path of fate it is essential to be aware that a change in attitude is typically caused by an event that occurs in your the course of life. Anyone who regards their way of life meaningful is unlikely to have any desire to alter their outlook as opposed to someone who's facing difficulties or problems since he or she is more likely to rethink situation and could cause them to take a step towards change.

Passive and Active Hand

*If the line on the hands of the active is more clear and more distinct than that in the passive hand, this indicates that the person is meticulously planning their career path and goals throughout their life and has have a higher probability of success.

• If the line drawn in the active hand isn't clearly or well-marked compared for the passive hand, then the situation will be reversed.

Timing of Events

The process of determining the line of fate is much simpler because there is no curve in it when compared to other important lines that run through the palm. Distance from the top Mount of Saturn to the base of the palm is seventy years.

After you've taken a measurement of the distance, you may make use of a small set of dividers in order to determine the period of time one decade at an time. A line's length must divide by 7ty, and multiplied by 10 is equivalent in the length of 10 years.

You could also determine the distance that is occupied by every year by dividing the length by seventy in order to determine the date of your subject's occasion (Length of the heart's line divided by seventy equals year). Then you can determine your distance between the peak Mount Saturn Mount of Saturn to the area you're interested in, then divide this measurement in the number of years, and then subtract the results from the figure of seventy. (Apex of Saturn to the point of attraction = distance. Distance divided by years (years from 7 years. Seventy years minus seventy = the age of the event.)

However, just like other lines, the exact date or time of any event is not exact. Even experts in palmistry can only estimate the year of any marking or alteration in the line of fate.

Chapter 8: The Line Of Success

When you think about the line of achievement, also known by"the Line of Apollo, the crucial thing to consider is that it is a sign of success from the perspective of an individual, not from a worldly view or the way society defines success. Therefore, it could be regarded as the personal line of success. If you notice this mark on the wrist of your subject , it means that they are able to lead the life they wish to lead and are also able to perform actions that show their personal identity.

There are times when you see people with an established success rate but has achieved great success or have become very prosperous to the extent where they're receiving international recognition for their accomplishments. In these instances regardless of the degree of success these individuals have and how much satisfaction they be feeling from their achievements however, their lack of a line from Apollo suggests that they don't have the level of success they'd like to attain and can't lead the life they'd like to live, as if they weren't able to achieve the life they desire in their own way. In contrast someone who earns a decent living doing what they like to do will likely be satisfied with their life and that is evident by the lines of Apollo written onto their hands.

General Information on Line of Success Line of Success

If the line of success is more clear, deeper with well-marked lines, that suggests an increased degree of personal achievement. But it's the relative quality of the line that needs to be taken into consideration.

In the event that the line is clearly drawn, clearly marked and very obvious, your subject may be sure to enjoy a high amount of personal accomplishment. In reality, they will be destined to achieve fame and recognition. However If your lines from Apollo are thin and weak or are fading they indicate a lower level of personal accomplishment.

A palmist can establish or even gauge how old a person is when the feelings of personal achievement begin by examining the starting location in the Apollo line. The line is often not visible at a high point in the hand, indicating that it takes a lot of time for a person to grow their lives to the stage where they are able to feel successful personally.

If a palmist sees lines that start at the bottom of the hand, this means that the individual has experienced some sort of personal success in a relatively young age, either through some sort of luck, or perhaps with the help of other people. In the majority of cases the palmists will see the line as thin and starts high on the hand , which generally indicates that someone can only accomplish the things they would like to accomplish and lead the life they wish to lead after having retired.

If you notice a one vertical line that is clearly and clearly marked upon the mount of Apollo it is usually a sign that, regardless of how artistic or creative a person might be as the line appears solely on the mount Apollo They won't be successful until later in life.

When the success line is at Upper Mars, it indicates that the success eventually is a result of a relentless determination. Your subject will probably have repeatedly try and experience many failures before they achieve what they desire in life.

If you notice an crossbar, dot, or island in the direction of Apollo generally indicates that the person is going to go through one or more challenges before they achieve personal success.

An island is a prolonged time of trouble A dot is abrupt and unplanned while a crossbar displays the presence of an interference. Similar to the problems in any other line character of the line that is successful following a fault is to be assessed to determine whether the problem has lasting effect on the individual or the subject.

If you spot a clearly marked star along the lines of Apollo the phenomenon is generally believed to indicate fame and prosperity, however only a few have the sort of success and recognition that they hope for.

If there's no fate line that your subject has in his hand The line of Apollo could compensate for that however it is usually a sign that the person is spending their life in the present or in the moment, doing things that they enjoy rather instead of thinking about the future. If you find that the line drawn by Apollo is stronger, it means that their motivation to do what they would like to accomplish and live the life they wish to lead is greater in comparison to their need to keep building their lives along the desired lines of the destiny line.

If the path of fate is stronger than the other two, it indicates that even though the desire of a person to build their life according to intended path is accompanied by a sense of personal achievement however, they do not have the same sense of personal success as they would like.

When the line from Apollo runs toward Saturn it is usually a sign that your subject is trying to make use of their own success to promote something that they believe in and which is important to them.

Timing of Events

The method utilized to determine the timing of events within the lines of failure, or that of Apollo is exactly similar to measuring the line of destiny. Distance from the top on the Mount of Apollo to the base of the palm is seventy years , and the marks can all be measured by using the same method described in the chapter on The line of destiny (see the previous chapter).

Chapter 9: A Look At The Line Of Marriage And Children

Modern and traditional palmists have observed their traditional interpretations for these signs are highly uncertain, and it's very difficult to pinpoint precisely and precisely when a person will be married, or have children, or the number of children they'll have. They say that couples get married and have children for various reasons.

That's why the majority of palmists try to figure out the reason why their client will be married initially Is it because they love their partneror because of other personal motives? Perhaps they are looking to have children. This will allow them to be aware of which part of the hand is to be read by.

While there are numerous instances where the marriage line can be accurately translated into a real-life wedding, there's plenty of cases where it does not. If it does happen you could say it's luck or an unlucky coincidence on the palmist's side since most times, reality does not correspond to the number of marriage lines in their person's hands.

Lines for Marriage Lines

Marriage lines are small lines that run along the side of the hand below the pinkie finger, and above the heart's line. They could also be lengthy lines that extend from the side to the Mount of Mercury and sometimes extends into the palm. These lines suggest that a person communicates with the other person in a particular manner.

When the line of marriage is clearly marked, it indicates that there is a higher degree of communication. Also, if the lines are strong and distinct, this generally suggests a close relationship.

If the depth line falls located close to the line of love it suggests that a couple will be married in the early years of their lives.

Happy marriage lines must be straight and unambiguous, without islands or splits within it. The lines are often at the top of Mercury.

If the line is curving downwards your subject will outlive the spouse or partner of his/her choice.

If the line moves upwards in reverse the couple may not be married.

If your line appears straight but there are lines of drooping this could indicate problems in the marriage due to an illness.

If the line appears clearly marked, but breaks in two places, it could signal the possibility of a break-up or even a death in a happy, happy marriage.

If the line of marriage is joined by the sun's line or the line of success typically signifies that the person being married will marry someone wealthy or has a form of distinction. If, however, the same type of line is bent and cuts across the lines of the successful, this means that the person is unable to be a part of the wedding he/she is planning to have.

In the event that the line Mercury runs into the marriage line it suggests that there'll be a lot of obstacles to the marriage, which need to be overcame.

If lines cross the Mount of Mars and then climbs to the wedding line, it usually suggests that there will be conflicts within the wedding.

Islands

If you see an island when you first start this usually means that the wedding will be delayed for quite a long time . They may be separated for the course of their married life. One example is when the spouse is employed abroad or is located far away.

If the island lies in the middle of the marriage continuum this indicates that a divorce will likely take place during the course of their marriage.

If the island is at the edge in marriage suggests that the marriage is likely to have an unlucky endings as well as the separation.

If the marriage line comprises of tiny chains or islands and the couple is cautioned not to marry anytime soon, as the marriage is likely to be a source of discontent.

Fork Lines

If the marriage line splits into a fork couples will most likely remain apart, but should the fork be turned towards the direction of the heart, a legal separation could take place.

The fork's line gets accentuated and one side of the fork extends toward the mountain of Mars the marriage may end with divorce.

But what a palmists are unable to say or decide is whether the relationship is sexual, romantic, or perhaps just platonic.

In such matters to be dealt with carefully because people are sensitive to their relationship and love An individual may inform you about their relationship, however they are not likely to discuss other aspects of their past relationships or affairs, or even those they loved and cared for, but did not engage in. The complexity of close relationships are challenging and non-reliable. You should be honest with your partner when you're unable to comprehend or understand your spouse's marriage line.

You may also reference the line of fate in previous chapters as it is linked to love and affection.

Children Lines

These lines are very unstable, and so that the majority of palmists who are competent avoid them entirely. While there are instances where, in the case that of an elderly person the lines of children's numbers accurately correspond to the number of children they've experienced, such instances are extremely rare. Learning is a continuous process and , over time it is possible for new information to enable a palmist to tackle the issue of children more precisely however, for the moment it is better for the student to stay away from using these lines to determine the amount of children one has.

The lines that relate to children are located over the marriage line. They are usually clean and precise straight lines. These lines are clearly marked and are typically seen more in women than males.

When the lines appear wide and deep, it typically indicates children, however if the lines are thin and narrow the couple is likely to have daughters.

If the line is straight, this will generally indicates healthy and strong children, however If the lines are bent or are almost faded indicates that the kids are extremely sensitive with their overall health.

If the little lines contain tiny areas, the kid may develop illness at an early stage, however should the line become well-marked beyond these islands and the child is ill, then he/she will improve and become stronger or, more likely, recover. If the line is damaged or is ending which could indicate that the child is not going to develop, which implies that the child may die in the future.

If any of the lines stands out, or is more prominent than other lines, it means the child is more important to parents, or will have more success than those around him/her.

Chapter 10: The Minor Marks And The Conclusion

Once you've mastered the signs of the main lines on the palm in this chapter, you will get information on the meanings of different markings that can be found on the lines as well as on the various mounts. Additionally, you will be provided with some suggestions on what to do prior to letting your student begin to analyze the palm in order to get the most accurate reading and to be on the way to becoming an expert palm reader.

The Circle

A circle on the palm is very rare when you see an object with a circular marking on their hands it is a sign of undesirable or unfortunate situations. A lot of palmists view it as to be a negative sign, but when it's found on the surface or the Sun it could be considered to be positive.

If the circle's mark is in contact with any lines or mount, it typically indicates the opposite or a negative outcome to the line it touches or crosses. In palmistry, circles generally signify an ongoing situation from which can't be easily escaped or escape from. When the circular area is on the Mount or the mount of Moon or on the mount of Luna one could drown.

The Spot Spot

Spots usually signify the presence of a chronic illness or. If the mark touches an area, it is a sign that an illness that is temporary can manifest.

If the area is on the forehead it could be a sign of head trauma or shock. If the spot crosses that line, it indicates a sudden illness when it's situated near that line, it signifies fever. It is usually not of any importance if the area is situated on the other lines on the palm.

The Grille

According to many palmists grille marks are the area at which energy is released, therefore when you see grille marks on the hand or even the whole palm, it's usually an indication that the person's power and energy is constantly depleted and could also be dissipating.

If the grille mark is in contact with any of the mounts, it depletes the vitality of the particular mount. This also means that the individual will go many challenges in their lives which are related to the specific mountain it touches, or symbolizes. One example is that the case where the grille is discovered at the top of the mount Apollo There will be a no success in the merits of the mount it represents.

The Star

The star is usually a wonderful symbol as it symbolizes excellence and the best things in the life of a person.

If a line has the ending of the shape of a star, it typically suggests that the person will be the most successful person in their life. But, as says the old saying, "success always comes with an expense." The symbol of the star can also mean that it is accompanied by the cost of a bad experience.

If it is located on the Mount of Jupiter It means power, glory and possession.

If it is located on the mountain of the Sun it will bring wealth and glory even though it is usually associated with the public realm.

If it's located on the side of Mercury this means you will have the ability to succeed in business or corporate projects, scientific or scientific pursuits depending on other signs.

If it's located at the foot of Mars which is located under the Mount of Jupiter this means that the individual will be able to make significant distinction in their marital life or is going to be involved in a fight which will increase the prestige of his/her profession.

If it's on the Mount of Mars which is located under the Mount of Mercury It usually confers the honor of winning by overcoming one's own life or by having to conquer personal difficulties.

If it's located on the moon/luna mount It's a signification of fame and acclaim that is based on the quality that the mountain.

When the star can be situated on the mountain of Saturn typically, it indicates adverse circumstances for someone's life. It can be a sign of distinction however it is one to be feared. The person you are describing is portrayed as one of the tragic events of life. The person's life is likely to result in tragedy or an extremely tragic event that causes the name of the person to be remembered, or to have an image, but for unlucky reasons. One example is a king who was crowned by a doom.

The Cross

A cross usually signifies an indication of danger, the danger of or discontent. If it's on lines, certain palmists suggest that the bearer has burdens that are similar to those of those of the Holy Cross of Jesus. It could also refer to the occurrence of a major shift in one's lifestyle because of a tragedy, crisis incident, or difficulties.

The only good sign of a cross when it is located in the Himmelsrath of Jupiter. This indicates that the person is exceptionally fortunate in the friendship that will blossom in the life of his/her partner. If it's on other mounts, it indicates unfavorable conditions.

The person could end up in a brutal death in the event that the sign is located in the direction of Saturn.

There will be disappointment with fortune or money if it's found on the equator of the Sun.

Dishonesty is likely to occur if it's is found on the Mount of Mercury.

It will be a great challenge in the case of Mount Mars which is situated beneath the Mount of Mercury.

If it's located on that mount Mars underneath that of Jupiter It usually signifies an unsettling death due to disputes.

If a cross appears on the Mount of Luna this signifies that someone will be deceived and result in a fatal impact on one's imagination. When the cross can be located on the lower portion of the mountain, this is a sign of drowning death.

If the cross is located on the mountain of Venus this means that there's some negative influence that is connected to affections.

If the crossing is located above the line of the head It could indicate an accident or head injury.

If the cross sits higher than the line of the heart, this indicates the sudden death of a loved one.

The Square

The square, which is also known as the symbol of Preservation It is an ideal symbol as it protects you from unlucky signs that result from my chain, broken or dotted lines on the palm. While problems will likely be encountered, the person who holds it is able to prevent the situation and damage is minimized or prevented.

If it's found on the line of life, this means the preservation of life, and when it is located along the destiny line it will be preserved from loss, based upon the condition of the line and the indications it gives.

The Triangle

Another positive symbol is the triangle as it usually indicates the strength (if it's an independent mark and doesn't contain connecting lines). It is made up of the head, the life line and heart lines. It is usually a sign of the health and mental well-being of a person as well as achievement based on the line or the mount it crosses.

If it's at the top of the island of Apollo It is an indication of artistic achievement. The bigger the triangle, more successful dependent on the lines or mounts that it is affixed to. Triangles also symbolize balance and they do not carry backlash like stars.

The Quadrangle

It is a place that is located between midway between the line of the head and the heart, which is an arc or quadrangle. A quadrangle that is well-defined must be formed evenly , and shouldn't have a narrow edge on all four corners. It is also a reflection of an individual's mindset towards others.

Quadrangles signify balance in mind and judgement. If it's extremely narrow, it is a sign of narrowness regarding their religious beliefs. However when it's too broad, it indicates the lack of judgement, and a sloppy view of the good of one's fellow man.

Some Guidelines to follow before reading the Palm

After you've learned the basics of palmistry and all of its different indications the most important thing to learn in order to ensure you get the most effective outcomes is to ensure that the palm of your subject prepared and "prepared" prior to the time you are able to clearly read it. Here are some guidelines that will assist you in preparing yourself and the palm of your subject.

* If you can avoid touching the hands of your subject prior to when you conduct any reading of the palm. Don't touch them with your hands or before you examine them because the electrical energy of your body could alter the actual characteristics of the hands and palm.

* You can look at the palm any time during the day, however most experts suggest that the ideal moment to look at it is early in the

168

day, after breakfast, or prior to when doing anything important. The reason is because the digestion of food can affect the circulation of blood and as a result, minor lines can be invisible following food intake or intense activities.

* It's also ideal to ensure that your subject as well as you, the person who reads palms took a bath before performing palmistry. This will help avoid stumbling blocks in interpretation because the body that is dirty or uninvolved is a huge distraction to the surroundings.

Palm readers should never look at a palm that is either extremely cold or hot temperature because of weather changes. The hand is likely to alter its color based on the weather conditions outside that can impact the reading.

* Individuals shouldn't visit a doctor for a test in the event that they have consumed alcohol, or any other intoxicants like drugs, etc. or if the person has a bad mood or is in good health. That's why, as an expert in palms, you must discuss your subject with them first. You should get familiar with

them or ask them about their experience before or what made them decide to see you. It is also possible to go through a list of questions you need to ask your subjects to ensure not to miss everything.

An experienced palmist ought to not give any readings when he/she is upset or unhappy or in poor place.

As an expert in palms, you must be sure to examine your hand with the greatest care. Even if the person is a close friend, loved one , or even an adversary. Don't let your emotions overrule the fundamental readings of palmistry Otherwise, your predictions are most likely to be flimsy. Say it the way you see the situation, but don't conceal the truth. And like the majority of things in life do not let your emotions affect your judgment, or in this instance your interpretations.

Chapter 11: Understanding Palmistry

In the first section, we are devoted to a general understanding of the process of palmistry. Before we discuss its procedure or method it is important to understand the subject's scope first. A lot of people get confused as to what a palmist is able to do and not and how the palmistry process works all over the world, based on the information they've read in publications, newspapers social media, or online blogs, or have been told from different stories told from one family member to another regarding predictions for the future and the process the process of reading palms. These are the main reasons for confusion due to the fact that our minds tend to form opinions or opinions from what we read, perceive or hear. For the majority of people, palmistry can be a notion that seems a bit unrealistic.

It is difficult to tell the truth about whether it is working or not, as there are instances or circumstances where it is possible to claim that it is in connection with the words written on a palm (based upon the interpretation of the expert or palmist) However, there is no way to prove that it actually works. It's not so much a matter of whether it's effective or it doesn't. It's more about whether one believes in that or not. That is why having an open-minded mind essential particularly if you want to be a skilled palmist.

What exactly is Palmistry?

Chiromancy, or palmistry, is the analysis and interpretation of human palms. Palmists or palm readers generally examine hands and fingers of their customers or subjects and do a thorough study of the various aspects of the hand and, from that, draw possible meanings based on the rules and structures of palmistry.

There are numerous aspects to be considered before performing an effective palm reading. typically, experts will identify the character of the person they're trying read. It is about knowing the character, personality mentality, physical features such as sexuality, background, along with other important elements like the uniqueness and features of the fingers and hands. Each hand is distinctive, and each tells its own story. Like fingerprints, you will never discover the same fingerprints because every person that has ever lived is unique, and perhaps that is the reason we are human. There might be some similarities in designs, but it's not exactly the identical. Even if two people have the exact same handprint certain they are from different backgrounds and possess a distinct personalities, which could alter the meanings of their hands completely.

Every pair of hands for each person is distinct; you can't have the same handprint for your right and left hands that's why it is important to treat each hand as an individual. If a palmist claims that they know when a person is likely to be married and have children or when somebody die, they are most likely to be a fraud or scammer because they've lost touch with reality and become optimistic already. True palmists or skilled reader shouldn't claim anything. You can easily determine whether they're competent or not, based on the amount of years working in the field, or how they analyze all information before making any conclusions or conclusions.

Despite its long history however, it's still relatively new and has a lot of potential aspects to be explored. According to some experts, palmistry is a method to treat mental illnesses or mental disorders due to the way it works is to explore a person's internal self to uncover one's inner conflicts and draw predictions from the underlying issues. It's basically the same as the work that psychologists or mental therapists provide to patients to enable them to reconnect with his/her inner self in order to address the root of problems. Palmistry is one of the therapies that can help cure mental illness in the future according to certain experts.

The future will only be determined by the time palmistry proves to be useful instrument for mental health, and may someday be a an integral part of the future of psychology. There's a long way from that happening however, like all things, it's an option. However, if you're keen to dive into the unknownand wrestling with the complexities of human nature, palmistry could help you begin your journey.

How do you differentiate Palm Readers from Frauds?

There is a vast distinction between being aware of something and using what you have learned. The way you approach the subject matter is of vital importance. That's why the application of information on all aspects related to palmistry is important since it can benefit you in particular when your subject or client asks questions or inquires regarding the differences between what you stated in your readings from the past to the current readings.

Customers , especially those who do not be convinced of this practice will certainly be skeptical about the accuracy of the accuracy of your reading. That's the reason you should be able to differentiate yourself from fraudulent palmists or at least understand the various "types" of readers so that are able to determine the type of reader or palmist you want to be.

Technical Palm Readeror Scientific Hand Analyst

The technical palm reader is the type of palmists who study and evaluate each aspect of the hand. Every word they speak of has an origin and is arranged by the rules of palmistry. Technical palm readers can make some educated guesses or hypotheses occasionally, however, it's still based on many factors like hands, fingers lines, mounts, and so on. They do not make claims solely on the basis of their gut intuition, all of it is weighed into the framework that they work. One way to determine whether a palmist has technically skilled is if they are able to clarify the claims they made and at the same time provide a clear explanation or pinpoint the palm of the person who gave them on how they came up from a certain belief. They are identified as technical analysts.

Clairvoyant or Psychic Palm Reader

The term "psychic" means "palmist," but it doesn't mean they are experts. In fact, they might not be completely knowledgeable about the art of palmistry. The majority of clairvoyant readers use their senses to predict the future in a short-term manner and make this happen by using an individual's palm the central point or instrument of their ability to determine their client's current and future. If, for any reason, you've had the experience of visiting a psychic prior to but then changed to a more technical palm reader, they could not give you a specific explanation or clarify how they was able to come up with the prior reading due to different methods.

Card Readers

Card readers can predict a person's future using Tarot cards. It's simple: they advise clients to shake their cards. They then cut it , and distribute it with a variety of mysterious design. Each card has its own significance, but there are certain card readers who mix the traditional interpretation of cards together with their 'psychic' or intuitive skills to forecast their

At the time of the antiquated Greeks and Romans the practice of palmistry was thought of as a scientific discipline. Famous figures like Hypocrites, Galen and Julius Caesar philosophers, philosophers as well as warriors, have studied this as if it were an important area of study. It was in the past. Numerous scholars and religious leaders discussed the academic nature of palmistry. The debate concluded in a positive manner as many books were published regarding palmistry line reading but because of the growth of Christianity and palmistry, as well as other similar practices was deemed an heresy since it is not based on any evidence-based basis and is not a sound idea.

Medieval Era

In medieval times the art of reading palms was banned by the Church because certain religious people saw the practice to be "black witchcraft," after all no one other than God knows for sure what the future will bring. There are certain people who were so enthralled by the act, only to end getting beaten to death. In the past those who were practicing palm reading were considered to be 'wizards.' Palmistry is proclaimed as witchcraft and a weapon of the devil. And many who practiced it were tossed off a mountain and killed in pain. However, due to the arduous handling of this method, many throughout the years were interested and more open to reading the palms of their hands. The practice eventually gained traction and is still in use to this today.

Present Day Palmistry

In the years that followed the church's chiromancy laws have weakened as the world is more open than ever before to diverse ideas and different beliefs. Palmistry and its fundamental information have been passed on from generation to generation and gained acceptance in several nations, and eventually became a profession of honor for certain people. Many people take it up to have enjoyment or for a hobby and some people who believe in it are so open, they relate everything that happens within their lives or their future with their palms have revealed. If you are a believer or not in the science behind Palm readings, I believe

we can all acknowledge that it's fascinating
to research and study.

Conclusion

Palmistry was probably invented or discovered as a method to convince people to be convinced of something which could increase their expectations and encourage them to hope of a better future. Perhaps it also is a way to warn people and give the public a glimpse of what's in store for them, and the negative consequences. Whatever the interpretation make sure to remember that the future has not yet written. It could alter for the better or worse. Moreover, although the practice is completely untested, I think palmistry has a purpose to keep people in mind and give that one thing: your future lies in your hands!

CPSIA information can be obtained
at www.ICGtesting.com
Printed in the USA
BVHW050501070223
658033BV00008B/127